C000131981

# IT'S FUNNY BEING ME

– ROY 'CHUBBY' BROWN –
with Steve Cowper

An environmentally friendly book printed and bound in England by
www.printondemand-worldwide.com

 **Mixed Sources**
Product group from well-managed
forests, and other controlled sources
**FSC** www.fsc.org Cert no. TT-COC-002641
© 1996 Forest Stewardship Council

 **PEFC**
PEFC/16-33-415

PEFC Certified
This product is
from sustainably
managed forests
and controlled
sources
www.pefc.org

This book is made entirely of chain-of-custody materials

www.fast-print.net/store.php

It's Funny Being Me
Copyright © Roy 'Chubby' Brown and Steve Cowper 2011

Management – Stuart Littlewood for Handshake Ltd
www.handshakegroup.com

Website – www.chubbybrown.biz

Cover photographs – Andy Hollingworth

Special thanks to Andy Wood for his help in putting this book together

ISBN 978-178035-220-6

First published 2011 by
FASTPRINT PUBLISHING
Peterborough, England.

# *Foreword*

Well, here we go again, I've written another book and this will be one of those that when you pick it up, you'll begin to regret it. You see, I don't read books; I read the Sun newspaper. Actually, that's a lie; because when I get to page three I can't let go of my cock, so I can't turn the pages.

I have a few things to tell you before you read this book. Firstly, if you don't like it, it is carefully designed to fit under the leg of a wobbly coffee table. If you don't have a wobbly coffee table, it will make a great addition to your bonfire on 5th November.

Anyway, since the last book, I've been doing really well, and I've had my photo taken more times than William and Kate, mainly due to those camera phones and a couple of police stations. But, despite all this, I'm still doing my "One Man Show," and I keep hoping that maybe a couple more will turn up to see the next one.

On a more serious note, I want to thank everyone who sent me cards and e-mails after my battle with cancer. It's those that kept me going when I felt like giving up. I mean with a doctor like mine, you have to worry. He asks you to hold his balls when you cough! Once, when I told him I couldn't piss, he said, "Chubby, you're sixty six, don't you think you've pissed enough!"

I'm getting older, and they've just cancelled "Last of The Summer Wine," so bang goes one of the few acting roles that would have suited me. So I decided to try to become a "Pin Up Boy" but unfortunately, they didn't have enough pins to keep me up. But at least my memory is good, and I can remember everything, which is good because I've seen more sex than a copper's torch. In fact I've been in more intimate places than a hard-core porno camera.

When I wrote the first book, the wife was frightened that I might disclose some of our intimate secrets, like the fact that she doesn't clean her teeth after eating one of my pies. Or should that be the other way round? She was a bag of nerves, which shocked me because normally she's just a bag.

It's a fact that in this business, you don't get anywhere without a good agent. If the agent likes you, they find it easier to "sell" you and they have to convince all the other agents to book you. I have worked for agents where I have had to camp outside their office to get my money. As for the venues, to say that they were like cowsheds would be unfair to cowsheds! Most of the Jewish agents looked like Groucho Marx, hence the drawing.

THE AGENT
Two for me one for you

One agent in Wales had a dog, and when you went to his office, the dog would sniff your balls and you would get embarrassed and walk out of the room without your money. It didn't work with me because when I grabbed it by its bollocks and twisted them, it soon backed off.

My current manager is so tight that his computer is in black and white. I'm sure he's had his office soundproofed so nobody can hear him saying, "Two for me, one for Chubby." I have to say, managers are a rare breed, but we do need them. You see, I could write my achievements on the back of a postage stamp before I got good management.

Anyway, it's time to start reading this, my second book. It isn't a second autobiography; it's more a collection of stories from my life. Some are funny, some are sad, but all are true. I hope you enjoy what you are about to read.

Roy "Chubby" Brown

# It's Funny Being Me

After being born at an early age, I was dragged up in one of the toughest areas in Middlesbrough. I have some great memories of those days, even though it was tough. As kids, we still had an innocence about us, and I clearly remember having pictures on my bedroom wall of the rock and roll stars of the day. But unlike today, they had all their clothes on. We didn't know about sex then, though I certainly made up for it later in life. However, when I was about 10 years old, my sister, Barbara, caught me groping Lillian Hardy's left tit. Being a girl, she said, "I'm telling our dad!" because that's what sisters did. I had to talk her out of it, but it's a good job she never found out about Lillian's best mate who was charging me a shilling to look at her fanny! Of course, my piggy bank was always empty; so I used to get up very early in the morning, sneak outside to go up and down the road pinching the milkman's money from underneath the bottles. I always made sure I had enough money for a glimpse of fanny and a feel of tit. Nothing really changes does it?

I may have mentioned (several times) that Grangetown was a typical North East industrial town. The local steelworks and other heavy industry polluted the air, but nobody bothered because they provided jobs for the people. I used to say that on a clear day, you could see for inches! The air was thick with coal dust and smog, and the generally damp atmosphere made it a very unhealthy place to grow up. But, on the plus side, people used to sit on their doorsteps and chat to each other. Extended families would live in the same street, and you were part of a community. That just doesn't happen today.

Our house was just a hundred yards from the railway line, so dad and I would regularly go over with buckets to pick up the coal that had fallen off the trucks. Well, I would pick up the coal whilst dad held the bucket. It was what everyone did back then, we had no money to spare, and so nicking the coal to keep us warm was a necessity. We were poor, and it really was like the old gag where the burglars broke into our house and left us £20.

It's sad to think that people died young in those days, but it's not surprising, as it was a very unhealthy lifestyle. The men worked in hot, sweaty factories amongst all the pollution. When they had finished for the day, they would be in the club, drinking and smoking to excess. It's hard to think that this was only sixty years ago. We had to develop a sense of humour to cope with life. In fact, I love the dictionary definition of the word joke. It says that a joke is something that excites or creates a laugh, which changes the expression on people's faces. I certainly enjoyed changing those expressions. I used to say that my sister wasn't carrying a bit of extra weight; she was fucking dragging it around! I told people that she was so big she'd come from an ostrich egg and not to invite her to a party; she'll drink the finger bowl. All joking aside, my sister is just like me; we've spent our lives trying to lose weight.

When we were kids, dad was very strict and wouldn't allow any messing about at the dinner table, no talking, and definitely no laughing. Of course, that was like a red rag to a bull and I would try to make her laugh as much as possible to get her into trouble. Dad was usually the target of my jokes, but he could be funny too. He would often talk to himself, and when he dropped a hammer on his foot, he shouted out, "Fuckin' Hell." Then he answered himself by saying, "Well I hope they do, because I'm not getting nothing here." He was quite witty, and I still have a plaque that he used to have above the fireplace. It read, "I drink to your health my old mate. I drink to you alone. I drank to your health so many times, I've practically ruined my own." He also had a favourite gag, which he must have told a thousand times. It was, "My mate's giving his wife too much money. When he got home the other night, there was a bloke stood in the wardrobe. Apparently, she had paid him to look after her clothes." I don't think I could get away with that one now.

# Schooldays

I must have been about nine years old when my dad made me a bogie. Kids today wouldn't know what one of those was, but we had great fun with them. Bogies were a sort of Go Kart, made from a wooden box fitted on top of a set of old pram wheels. We used to have string attached to the front set of wheels so that we could pull on them to steer. We would also use bits of wood to make somewhere for your feet to rest. My bogie was like a formula one car, and could reach speeds of over ten miles per hour! We would all ride them down hills, trying to go as fast as possible with no thought for health and safety. In fact, I ended up in hospital when I went down a hill, lost control and crashed straight through a fence. I needed stitches and had to stop in overnight for observations.

This wasn't the first time that I had been in hospital. When I was a kid, I had scarlet fever and was admitted to West Lane Hospital. I was on the children's ward, and there was a 17-year-old lad in the next bed. He was lusting after one of the young nurses, and on a night, she would put the screens around his bed. I could see through a gap in them, and clearly remember seeing the bed sheets going up and down like a whore's knickers. But being young, I just thought that they were playing some sort of a game.

Thinking back, some awful things happened in those days. We had a lad in our class called "Sparky." He had got himself into a bit of trouble, so his dad confiscated his bike and gave him a clip around the ear. Sadly, he drowned himself in Eston Reservoir. The school closed that day as a mark of respect. Mr. Atterton, the Headmaster, read something out about it in assembly. I remember that as if it was yesterday.

I was forever getting into trouble at school, and one morning in assembly, everyone was talking and making a noise. The teachers had just managed to get everyone quiet when Raymond Basset farted. It was one of the loudest farts that I had ever heard, and I said, "Will somebody catch that!" Everyone started laughing at me, and anyone would have thought that it was me who had farted. I was hauled out of the hall and battered by one of the teachers, but I daren't tell my dad about it, because he would have battered me as well.

I was part of a group of lads who used to hang around the back of the girls' toilets. There was a broken window and we could see in. You know what it was like when you were kids, seeing a girl having a piss was very funny to us. It wasn't so funny when we saw a girl changing a tampon though. We were all just innocent kids, and this left us confused.

Just around the corner from the school, there was a building site, which turned out to be The Magnet Hotel, a place that became an important part of my life. Isn't it funny how people's lives were so insular at that time? Everything happened within just a few miles radius of where they were born.

# The Empire

The old Empire Theatre in Middlesbrough used to have Saturday Matinee performances every week at 3.00pm. The big names of the day were people like Beryl Reid, Jimmy Jewel & Ben Wallace, Petula Clark and The King Brothers and they would all be on at The Empire at one time or another. My father loved seeing these shows, and he would take me along every week. I would meet him outside the Unity Club, where he was the Concert Secretary. He'd usually had a "couple of pints" and was in a good mood. We then caught the trolleybus to North Ormesby where we would get off and walk to The Empire.

I remember one Saturday afternoon above all the others. On the way there, dad had stopped at the market and bought some cherries. We arrived at the theatre and took our seats in the balcony. The show started, and dad was eating the cherries, and as he ate them, he spat the stones into the bag. Because he'd had his lunchtime drink, he was enjoying himself and he loved making me laugh. Obviously, the drink had loosened his inhibitions, and when the second act came on stage, he was ready to show how uninhibited he had become. It was a "Specialty" act, and when a man came on with an assistant who was wearing what looked like a very bad bathing costume, my dad got the giggles. There was a table on the stage which had ten little boxes placed on it. Each box had a door in it, and as the man opened the doors, a budgerigar came out of each of them to do a trick. One of them rode a small bike, another one lifted some dumbbells and after they had performed, they stood on a perch. The audience lapped it up, and clapped as each budgie did its party piece. When I looked at him, my dad had an evil glint in his eye and said, "Watch this." He took the empty brown paper bag that had had the cherries in, and blew it up. Then, he held it at arm's length and smacked it with his other hand. There was a loud bang, and cherry stones flew everywhere, but worse than that, the budgies took fright and flew off in all directions. I thought it was funny, but the usherette, who was a little old lady didn't, and she shone her torch at us and said, "OUT."

I looked at my dad, and he looked at me. We both saw the funny side of the situation and we were marched out of the theatre to the sound of the other audience members chanting, "OUT, OUT, OUT." It could have been really embarrassing, but under his breath, dad was singing, "If you're happy and you know it, clap your hands." I, of course, was clapping, but very quietly.

I seem to remember that we went to see dad's sister, Auntie Connie, after we had been thrown out of the theatre. I loved going to her house, because she was always baking. In fact, I blame her for making me fat because I couldn't resist her apple pies and scones and cakes etc. Her house always smelled of cooking, and nobody ever left there hungry. She was an amazing woman, and amongst other things, she used to take me swimming. She would talk to the other women who had brought their kids, and one day, whilst she wasn't looking at me, another kid pushed me into the pool. I was only about nine years old, and couldn't swim very well. I was struggling and waving my arms about trying not to drown. Amongst all the noise, I could hear Auntie Connie's voice saying, "That's it Roy, put your arm over, splash your feet, keep going, you're doing well." She didn't realize that I was nearly drowning; she thought I was learning to swim.

When I finally reached the side, I saw the kid who had pushed me in. "You little bastard." I said. But when I had got dressed, Connie told me off. She said, "You know Roy, you're never going to make friends with people by shouting abuse at them." If she could only see me now!

# *Tossed off*

Back when I was about eleven years old and still sexually ignorant, I used to play football with my mates on Mathews Field. It was well known locally, and it was like our own Ayresome Park (Middlesbrough F.C.'s home ground at that time.) We would meet up outside Sir William Worsley's Secondary Modern, which was where I sometimes attended school. Opposite, were some bungalows, and behind them, the local Catholic School. We would make our way through the bungalows, along past school and on to the field. We really shouldn't have been on there, but as there wasn't a fence, and it had several fully marked out football pitches, it was too much of an opportunity for us kids to miss.

On one particular day, six mates and me headed of to the field for a game of footy. I ended up in goal, and we were all having a great time. One of the lads took a shot at goal but the ball flew over my head and into the long grass. I went to look for it, and as I was looking, I came across a lad called Jackie Towel, whose brother, Alan was in my class. He was just lying there with his cock out, and next to him was a girl who had her hand on it. Like a fool, I innocently said, "What are you doing Jackie?" He replied, "I'm being Tossed Off!" I looked blank, as he continued, "Have you ever been Tossed Off?" I thought for a second, and said, "Well I was tossed off the bus for fucking about." He laughed and said, "Do you want her to toss you off after she's done me?" You have to remember how innocent I was at eleven years old, because I said, "No, I'm in goal." Looking back I can't believe I turned down the offer, as that would have been my first sexual encounter.

When I got home, my dad was making our tea, because by this time in my short life, my mother had already fucked off and left us to cope on our own. As we sat at the table, my dad asked me what I had been doing that day, so I told him about playing football on Mathews Field. Then I said, "Oh, and I saw Jackie Towel being Tossed Off." My dad had just taken a drink of hot tea; he spat it out just like they do in the cartoons! In what seemed like a seamless motion, he raised his arm and clattered me around my head. "Don't ever say that again," he said. I didn't understand what "Tossing Off" meant, but I quickly realised that it meant you got clattered around the ear. In fact even now if I ask the wife, she clatters me around the ear too!

Jackie Towel must have told everyone he knew at school about this incident, because everyone seemed to be pointing at me and laughing. It wasn't long before I found out what I had missed out on, and let me tell you, from that moment on I wouldn't be running back to be in goal as quickly as I did on that day.

Writing this story has reminded me of another time in my life when I stumbled on an intimate sexual moment. I was travelling back from a gig in my little red "Post Office" van. I was driving along the Sedgfield to Coxhoe road, when I broke down; I just sat there crying. Sorry, I really must stop putting these bad jokes in this book. It was the van that broke down, NOT me. As these were the days before mobile phones, I looked around for a phone box but there wasn't one anywhere nearby. Luckily, I was close to a brand new housing estate so I wandered over to it. As it was well after midnight, there were hardly any lights on, but one house was still lit up downstairs. I decided that I would have to knock on the door and ask to use their phone to call my mate, Terry, to ask him to pick me up. Well, I gently knocked on the front door, but nobody answered. I knocked a bit louder, trying not to wake the whole neighborhood, but there was still no answer. I wasn't giving up, so I made my way round to the back of the house and peered through the window where I was greeted by the sight of a hairy arse going up and down ten to the dozen and the sound of a woman screaming like she was being strangled.

I just stood there frozen to the spot looking at this bloke who was knee deep in pussy. I thought, "Should I knock on the window?" but decided against that when I realised how big this bloke was. I mean he could have killed me with his spit alone! So I went and sat on the wall and waited for them to finish.

About ten minutes later, the lights went off and they must have gone straight upstairs, because the bedroom light went on. I decided that I couldn't knock on the door now, so I headed back to the van but my luck didn't improve as there was a policeman stood next to it. "Good evening sir, where have you been?" he said. Thinking on my feet, I said, "I've been for a piss." Well, I didn't want to admit to being a Peeping Tom. He then asked where I had been earlier in the evening, so I explained that I was a comedian and was travelling home from a gig when I had broken down, so I was actually looking for a phone.

His eyes lit up as he realised that he might have caught a drink driver. I knew I was under the limit as I had only had one pint, but my arse still twitched like a rabbit's nose when he produced the Breathalyzer. I, of course, passed the test and he said I could get on my way, but as I explained to him, I couldn't go anywhere, as the van was completely dead. He offered to radio in to the station and get a breakdown garage to come out to me, for which I was very grateful.

Anyway, by the time they came out to me, got the van on to the flatbed truck and got me home, it was nearly 5.00am. The bill for this call-out and repair came to nearly £200, which was a fortune to me. I had only earned £35 for the gig, so it wasn't only that woman in the house who was screwed that night.

I have always been good at drawing, but I've never really pushed that side of me. I like drawing cartoons; and I have been encouraged to put some in this book.

# *Animals*

When I was a kid and we were living at 30 Essex Avenue. I asked my dad if I could paint the bathroom walls, as they were just a dull green colour. He agreed, but got a surprise when he saw what I had done. I had painted Mickey Mouse, Pluto and Donald Duck on them. I don't ever remember him saying anything to me at the time, but I think he was amazed at the results, and if we had any visitors to the house, he would take them up to the bathroom to show them what "Our Roy" had done.

It was in this bathroom, not long after I had done the paintings, that I saw a spider on the bathroom floor. I ran over in my bare feet to stamp on it, but I nearly broke my toe. It wasn't a spider, it was one of my mother's old brooches that had been in the bathroom cabinet and had fallen on to the floor. I think this might have been the start of my problems with living creatures. Don't get me wrong, I love them, but I'm just not that good with them.

One of my Aunties tells everyone the story about my goldfish and me. It was Christmas, and I was worried that the fish might be feeling the cold, so, I checked the water with my fingers, and sure enough, it was a bit on the chilly side. In my mind that meant that the fish must also be cold. I immediately went to the kitchen, brought the kettle and started pouring hot water into the bowl. The fish sort of exploded, and bits of him floated to the top. I cried my eyes out, but my family just laughed. I thought I was doing something good, but instead I became labelled for life as "The Goldfish Murderer."

We also had a tortoise, and naturally I was upset when it died. I dug a hole in the back garden and buried him, placing a small cross, made out of ice-lolly sticks, to mark the grave. The next morning, when I got up, I looked out of my bedroom window and there was our dog, Paddy, running around the garden with a muddy, lifeless tortoise in his mouth. The bastard had dug him up! That's not all; we had a budgie that used to fly around the room. Unfortunately, I left both the room door and the back door open and the budgie flew outside, never to be seen again.

Of course, animals can always get their own back on you. Around about 1964, I got a job as a waiter at a well-known Holiday Camp in Blackpool. I was always up for working extra hours to make extra money, and regularly worked at the swimming pool. Each week, they would have a Junior Talent Show around the pool, and I often got roped in as one of the judges. One particular show was on a beautiful summer's day. There were lots of people there, but as judges, we were the centre of attention. Out of the blue, a seagull opened its arse and dropped its load all over me. It scored a direct hit, and it looked like somebody had just poured a tub of ice cream over my jacket. Everyone laughed, except me. To this day, I'm convinced that it must have been one of my early pets that had been reincarnated as a seagull, and its sole mission in life was to search me out to crap on me for all the bad things that happened to the animals from my childhood.

Anyway, going back to my childhood, the radio was always playing in our house. I loved music, and Rock and Roll was my thing. When I was old enough, I was lucky enough to be able to see Jerry Lee Lewis, Little Richard, Marty Wilde and many more at The Astoria in Middlesbrough. These people seemed to come from a completely different world, and they had a big influence on me.

As I grew older, I liked to keep fit and attended self-defence classes at the Grangetown Boy's Club. It was June 1963 when the trainer (who also looked after the pub and club doors in the Middlesbrough area) asked if I would like a job for the evening. Well I jumped at the chance to earn a few bob and he sent me to The Astoria where I was to take the tickets and act as a doorman for that evening's show. There was a fiver in it for me, so I headed to the venue and waited. I had arrived quite early, and was waiting in the car park when a cream coloured coach with blacked-out windows pulled up. The door opened, and a bloke got off the coach, came over to me and asked where to go to get a decent cup of tea. He had a very strange accent, and certainly wasn't from our area. I told him to go over the railway crossing, where he would find Black Bet's Café. That was the place where everyone went because it had the best Juke Box in town. He thanked me and returned to the coach. After a couple of minutes, everyone got off and walked to the café.

Later that night, the show was in full swing, and I realised that the support band on stage, were the same guys who had gone to the café earlier. They were called The Beatles, and to be quite honest I didn't think much of them. They weren't that good. But, like most people, I loved what they became. Oh, and the guy who asked me for the directions that day? Well it was John Lennon!

Over the years, I became a huge John Lennon fan and, after his death, I travelled to New York, just to see The Dakota Building where he died. I got a shock when I asked the security guard where Lennon was when he was shot. He just looked down and pointed to the cobbles in the archway, I was literally stood where Mark Chapman had stood in those fateful moments. A shiver went down my spine, as I remembered that day back in 1963 when he had asked me where to get a decent cup of tea. I couldn't believe that a mad man like Mark Chapman could take the life of such a talented, peace-loving person.

It was those early gigs that got me hooked on seeing live bands and singers. Over the years, I have seen everyone from AC/DC to Barbra Streisand. Once I went to the NEC in Birmingham to see Whitney Houston. After the show, we met up backstage, and she invited me back to her hotel. We had a drink in the bar, and she took me up to her room where she licked cream off my body. I distinctly remember her saying, "Chubby, you are the greatest lover in the world." But just as she slipped her hand around my knackers, I woke up! I have used that dream many times, usually when I'm alone!

# Getting Plastered

I was about 17 when I got a job with a company called, "Darlington Installation." I was employed as a labourer, and worked with the plasterers. I considered myself hard-working and conscientious. I would get up at 6.00am to be at work by 7.00am. The first job of the day was to mix the plaster so it was ready for the plasterers to start work at 8.00am. What I did was important to the tradesmen, because they were paid on their work performance. The more plastering they did, the more they got paid. So I had to keep them supplied with freshly-mixed plaster.

One morning, I was up a ladder getting some supplies. Without warning, there was a loud crack and the ladder snapped. I came tumbling to the ground in a heap and was covered in all sorts of shit. The foreman, who didn't really like me, came running over and I expected him to check that I was OK, but no. He said, "What the fuck are you doing?" so I stated the obvious and said "The ladder broke." His reply wasn't very sympathetic, "It's a good job you didn't spill any of that plaster mix because if you had, it would have come out of your wages!" He turned and walked away. As I picked myself up of the ground, I saw red. I had just about had enough of this foreman's snide remarks, and was going to let him know how I felt. I grabbed the nearest thing to me, which just happened to be a bucket of plaster. I ran over and tipped it all over him leaving the bucket on his head. Then I punched the bucket and he went arse over tit.

After a short time, he got up and without any hesitation, he said, "Consider yourself sacked." I replied, "Aye, and fuck you too." I really wasn't bothered, because in those days jobs were ten a penny and you could find another one by the following day.

Now, when I see that advert on the telly where that bloke says, "I was sent to fit an alarm and they gave me the wrong ladder and I fell off it," I have to laugh, because when I fell off a ladder, I got sacked; he fell off a ladder and got several thousands of pounds in compensation. I mean, how thick was he to fall of a ladder, any stupid bastard can climb a ladder, it's easy. Oh, hang on a minute; I'm just going to find a ladder to fall off again, who do I put the compo claim in to?

# *I'm Not A Girl*

In the early 1960's, I joined the Merchant Navy, and the world was at my feet. I couldn't wait to get on the ship and set sail. I considered myself quite tough, and never gave seasickness a thought. Twenty-one days later, I was still calling God down the big white telephone. Or, to put it another way, throwing up in the toilet. It was so bad; I was coughing up blood. After the initial few days, the crew stopped making jokes about my lack of sea legs, and became very concerned about me. They said I would soon get my sea legs, but it was just a matter of time. I had never been as ill as that before, but eventually I came around and got used to it.

When we docked in America, we all went ashore. I was just a lad from Grangetown, and I had never seen a supermarket before. I walked around, looking at everything they had on sale. I was like a kid in a sweet shop. They even had a café within the shop, but they called it a "Soda Bar." Of course, nowadays, most of our supermarkets have cafes, but back then, we were used to corner shops like the one in Ronnie Barker's "Open All Hours." So, for the novelty, we decided to get a drink in the Soda Bar.

I should explain at this point, that I had long hair. It was typical of what young lads in the UK had at that time, but in America they all had military-style crew cuts, and were all very clean-living, wholesome American boys. The two guys who were serving us were no different. I was a bit shy and wasn't saying much. To be quite honest, I was still a bit overawed by the store and actually being in America. My mate from the ship, a lad called Salty, was chatting away to the lads, and after about twenty minutes, he turned to me and whispered, "Roy, they think you are a girl, it's your hair!" I looked up, and noticed they were looking at me. I thought, fuck me; I'm going to have to put a stop to this, so I spoke up and told them, in my deepest voice, that I was a boxer, with sixteen fights under my belt, with twelve knockouts. They looked shocked, and apologised for their mistake. It could have turned nasty, but to their credit, they calmed the situation, and we got on like a house on fire. They were interested to know about life in Britain, and our life at sea. In the end, we swapped names and addresses and I wrote to one of them. He was called Dalton, and we kept in contact for years. But you know how it is, and eventually we lost contact with each other. I often wonder what happened to him, and wonder what he would think about what I became.

# Sharks and Potatoes

You've heard the saying that a cat has nine lives, well I think I must be a cat because over the years, I have had some lucky escapes. You look back at events in your life and think how the hell am I still alive! One of these times was when I was in the Merchant Navy and we had docked in Portuguese East Africa, which is now known as Mozambique. I was on shore leave with my Middlesbrough shipmates, Billy Loadwick, Brian Salt and Ray Blenkinsop. The beaches out there were stunning, and that is where we headed for a day of relaxation.

It was idyllic, people were swimming in the sea, the sun was shining and we were there to have a good time and recharge our batteries. As we looked for the perfect spot to settle for the day, I noticed a local youth in a ramshackle old hut. He was taking money from people and giving them towels, so being good northerners, we swerved him and found a spot where we didn't have to pay; it was just twenty yards from the sea and was just like paradise to us. We didn't give the towel guy a second thought as we settled in for the day.

As the day went on, the sun got hotter and we decided that it was time for a swim. We were in and out of the water and having fun, and as our stretch of the sea had nobody else in it, we could be loud without upsetting anyone. It really was perfect. Then, out of the corner of my eye, I noticed the local youth running towards us. He was shouting, "Saia da agua, Tubaroes!" I said to my mates, "look at that cheeky bastard, he wants money off us for being on the beach" Then he started waving a red flag and repeating "Tubaroes!" We ignored him, but he still kept running towards us. I'd had enough, there was no way I was going to pay to swim in the sea, so I came out to meet him. He babbled on in Portuguese, and I was shouting back in English. Then, we had a breakthrough, he said "English?" and I nodded "Yes." He continued in broken English and said, "You not go in sea here, you go there." He pointed to an area of the sea that had marker buoys surrounding it. So I said, "We not pay you to swim in sea." By now he was getting quite worked up and in his best "broken English" he explained that the buoys marked the safe area. They showed where the shark net was, and we were outside that area. Apparently, the previous week, two people had been attacked and killed by sharks exactly where we were swimming. You can imagine how we felt, I mean, how stupid of us to not even look at the signs in our efforts to avoid paying to swim in the sea. If it hadn't been for that youth, I might not have been here to tell the tale. The moral of the story is always take notice of the locals.

One time when I did take notice of the locals was when our ship, "The King Malcolm," sailed through the Suez Canal. I was on deck watching as we carefully navigated down the canal. It was amazing, as in places we were only about twenty feet from the banks. As ships go both ways through the canal, there are wider places to allow each other to pass. We all had our cameras out, and were taking photos. As I looked further down the banks, I saw a sight that I'd never seen outside of the movies, a "chain gang." They were digging at the side of the canal and were being watched over by armed guards on horseback.

As we watch on in amazement, two of the prisoners were allowed down to the side of the canal, where they proceeded to lift up what I can only describe as, similar to nightdresses. They then squatted over the edge and started to have a shit! Well, I was always mischievous, so I ran downstairs to the galley and brought back a load of old potatoes. We then started throwing them at "the shitters." I clearly remember hitting one of them right on his arse. He let out a scream, and we all laughed. Suddenly, all hell broke loose as the guards started shouting at us, and even fired a warning shot over our heads. This caught the attention of our captain who lined us all up for a bollocking. As if that wasn't enough, a boarding party came aboard to make an official complaint. After delicate negotiations, our Captain managed to smooth things over with them, but he was fuming with us. He gathered us all together and read us the riot act. We all received a "DN" stamp in our Seaman's Record Books, which is the equivalent of points on your driving licence.

On our return to Middlesbrough, we had to report to the Federation Office for a disciplinary hearing. We were lined up like naughty schoolchildren in front of a headmaster. The charge against us was "Throwing potatoes at an Egyptian prisoner's arse!" Even the disciplinary board had to laugh. I'm sure that they have never had to deal with a charge like that again. I still laugh when I think about this.

# *Scarborough*

It's well known that I was a "bit of a lad," and that I did a "bit of time." I soon learned that to survive, you had to be tough. So, I became the type to use my fists first and ask questions later.

In the months before I got sent down, I had been living and working in Scarborough. Now, I've always liked a fuck, and was always on the lookout for my next conquest. It was 1962, and I was working as a waiter at The Southlands Hotel. I fancied this pretty girl who worked in the kitchens, but she seemed a bit on the shy side, and she never seemed to talk to anyone. She was called Chris, and her mother was a cook at the hotel. It took a while for me to find out that she wasn't shy; she was actually deaf and dumb.

One day, totally out of the blue, her mother cornered me in the kitchen. I thought she was going to proposition me, but no, she asked me if I would take Chris out on a date. Apparently, Chris really fancied me, but surprisingly, couldn't tell me! My first thought was, "Fuck me, what would we talk about?" then I realised that was a stupid thing to think! She was actually quite tasty, so I agreed, and told her mother that I would take her for a walk down on the beach, and would look after her.

We set off, and by the time we had reached the South Bay beach, I was getting a bit pissed off as we couldn't talk to each other. I had all the patter, and knew how to get into girls' knickers, but this was totally out of my comfort zone. We walked along by the amusement arcades, and as we reached the public bogs, she made the gestures that she wanted a piss. So, I stopped and pointed to the "ladies," she smiled and grabbed hold of my arm, and pulled me in to the toilets, and straight into a cubicle. She snogged my face off, and the rest I'll leave to your imagination! I must admit that I was a bit shocked, but a fuck's a fuck.

When we got back to the hotel, her mother asked how things had gone, and what we had got up to. I couldn't tell her the truth, so I just said we'd had a "nice" time. I did think about learning sign language, but then thought it would be a lot of work just to get my end away, so I didn't take her out again. I know; I'm a right bastard at times.

# Dec and The Demon Drink

My cousin Derek, or Dec as he was known, was the first person to give me a chance as a drummer. He was a fantastic bass player and he toured with many of the country's top musicians. He also worked with the Joe Boston Jazz Ensemble, which was made up of some of the best jazz players in the UK. He even spent time working in Johannesburg, South Africa. I really looked up to him. Even today, people come up to me just to talk about him, and how good he was.

Unfortunately, Dec loved the "Rock and Roll" lifestyle. Sadly for him, playing in professional bands seemed to go hand in hand with drinking, and that's what killed him. I loved Dec, but I was permanently at my wit's end with him; he was so unpredictable when he was on the drink. Eventually, things became so bad, the doctor sent him in to the Memorial Hospital in Darlington for treatment. By this time, his kidneys were failing, and he was on medication to keep them going. I went to see him, and he was in a bad way. His eyes were yellow and his skin was all blotchy. But by this time, there was no turning back; I knew as soon as he got out of hospital he would be straight into the pub. It was heartbreaking, and as much as I tried, I couldn't help him.

When you know people like this, things happen which at the time are really bad, but when you look back, they were quite funny. One of these occasions was the time I got a call from the hospital saying that Dec had gone missing and that they had called the police to look for him. I asked to be kept informed, as I was very worried about him. It wasn't long before I got a call to say they had found him on the platform of the railway station. Apparently, he was only wearing a pair of socks, baggy underpants and clutching a six-pack of Carlsberg Special Brew Lager. They were taking him back to the hospital and I rushed there to see him.

After he had been checked out medically, I was able to talk to him alone. I asked him where he was going. He told me that he was trying to get to London to see his kids. I said, "Dec, you hadn't got any clothes on!" He said, "I know, I was going to nick some from some a clothes line, but I couldn't find one!" I think that shows the state of his mind, and as I said, it was tragic at the time, but actually quite funny now.

I have a photograph of that early band on my mantelpiece at home, and Tony Morris (singer) is no longer with us, Dec Vasey has gone. Bob Gray, Kevin Hunt, also gone. It makes me think every time I look at it, that you only have one life to live, so live it the best as you can.

# *The Drunkest I've Ever Been*

On my 21st birthday, I was playing the drums with the "Tony Morris Band" in a pub called "The Oasis," on the Lakes Estate in Redcar. It started out so well, but soon degenerated into a drunken night. People kept buying me drinks, and every drink was different. I remember drinking rum and coke, rum and blackcurrant and pints of Newcastle Brown Ale, and there were many other combinations of alcoholic drinks. Lots of my mates were there, including another drummer called Kevin Hunt.

After the gig, we decided to carry on drinking, and head off into town. I say we, but I mean they, because by that time, I didn't really know where, or who I was. It was Kevin who filled in the blanks a few days later. Apparently, they had to help me along, because I couldn't walk in a straight line. As we reached the van, they took the decision to put me in through the back doors, as that was the easiest way to deal with me. They all piled into the front, and prepared to drive away. Just at this point, a Police car pulled into the street, and in a bit of a panic, we pulled away. But, just as our van accelerated, the back doors flew open, and I came tumbling out of the van, landing in a heap on the road. The lads stopped the van to see if I was OK, but by the time they had got out, there were already two policemen and an Alsatian dog stood looking at me. One of the coppers then said, "Where do you think you're going, Sonny Jim?" at which point, in my drunken state, I started laughing. Then, I took a deep breath, like you do when you've had a few drinks and want to act sober, and said, "Do you know, officer, them fucking conductresses! If you don't have the right fucking change, they just fucking chuck you off the fucking bus." I don't know what they said, but I didn't get locked up, and I don't know how I got home. But it is good to know your mates look after you when you're drunk, and that the Redcar Police have a sense of humour.

COPPER

# Coppers and Vans

I miss the old-fashioned copper who had a sarcastic sense of humour. You know the type, they're the ones that could keep order because they were fair, but firm and you were always a little bit frightened of them. I guess that you have to be of a certain age to remember them, as times have changed so much. In those days, they would give you a clip around the ear. If they did that now, they'd get sued.

One night, about half past midnight, I was driving along Stockton High Street in my old van. I was minding my own business, when I looked in the mirror and saw the dreaded blue flashing light behind me. I stopped, and the policeman got out of his car and walked all the way around my van. I wound my window down as he leaned towards me. "Now then, what do we have here," he said. "A Van," I proudly replied. He looked me in the eyes and said. "So that's what you have decided to call it is it?"

I was shitting myself. He then said, "And who owns this so called van?" to which I replied, "I do sir." He looked me up and down and said, "Ohhhhhh, so you're admitting to it then. Shall we do a short roadworthiness test? We'll start with the handbrake." This wasn't looking good for me, as I knew the handbrake didn't work. It did, however, still make that clicking sound as you pulled the handle up, so I made damn sure he heard that. He went to the back of the van, and with all the force he could muster, he pushed, but the van didn't budge an inch. He looked surprised, but what he didn't realise was that I had my foot on the brake pedal. This was mainly because the brake lights didn't work either. He returned to the window and said, "OK, so the handbrake works, shall we try the horn?" Unfortunately, that didn't work, so, thinking on my feet, I said, "Well it must have just gone off, cos it worked earlier," but he wasn't buying that and said, "What would you do if you came around a corner and somebody was stood in the road; open the window and shout BOO!" Then, he shone his torch at the tyre. "Well, who did we buy these from, Yul Brynner?" (Google him, he's BALD) "There's absolutely no tread on them." Well, the comedian in me came out as I said, "Are you sure officer, because there's a man in hospital at the moment. I passed him and he got 50 lashes off them!" I think I got out of the police station about half past six that morning.

Thinking back to those days reminds me of another story with another van. I was living in Grangetown, and as I have mentioned before, it was a bit of a tough area. We had a local "hard case," called "Tosher" Stokes who, to show everyone how hard he was, used to throw house bricks into the air and head them like a football. Well, one day, I came out of our house to find a yellow van parked in the front near our gate, and me being a cheeky git, I thought, "Who does he think he is, parking there?" and decided to move it. I tried pushing and shoving, but it wasn't going anywhere. So, I looked around and found a house brick nearby, (which should have got me thinking.) I picked it up, smashed the window, took the handbrake off and pushed the van down the road.

About an hour later, I bumped into "Tosher" and his mate, "Nobby" Graham. You have to remember that these were two of the hardest men in Grangetown, but I got on great with them. "Tosher" said, "Hi Roy, how are you?" I said, "I'm OK" and was just about to tell him about the yellow van when he said, "I'm looking for the bastard who smashed my window." I said what's that all about Tosh?" and he said, "I've just bought a second-hand yellow van, and some bastard has smashed the window in and pushed it down the road. When I find out who did it, I'll kill 'em. I left it outside your house last night cos I thought it'd be safe there. " I looked at him and said, "Oh no, I haven't seen it. You say you left it in our road, are you sure?" He never suspected a thing. Mind you, if he had suspected it was me, he really would have killed me; he was a bit of an animal. I think I had a bit of a lucky escape that day.

# *Meeting My Mother*

I am a bit of a bastard. I know that you might find that hard to believe, but it's true. I've done a lot of hard drinking, a lot of gambling and have ruined a lot of relationships. I've even been locked up for a while, and done some stupid things, but looking back now, I wouldn't change any of it because I am finally happy and contented. The path that I took in life brought me to where I am now and I like where I am.

In life, you always want what you can't have, and in my case, that included several women. One particular girl wouldn't have opened her legs for anybody, not even if she was playing the cello. I really fancied her, and I tried to get her drunk one night, but there was no way was she having any of it. She would not take a portion! She reminded me of Dusty Springfield with her dark, sexy eyes, but she was more like Mary Poppins with her prim and proper ways. I did take her out, and after I had been seeing her for a few weeks, I thought I would take her to meet my mother. Now I'd only just got back in touch with my mother after many years apart. She was living in Wilton Avenue, Dormanstown and we were just getting to know each other again.

As soon as we walked in to the house, my mother sat us both down, but before I could say anything, she started to speak. "How long have you know our Roy?" but before the poor girl could answer, my mother carried on. "You know he's been married before and has two kids. Oh and he's been in prison! He's always drinking and he's never out of the bookies." I stopped her going any further and butted in saying, "OK mother, I think we've got the facts. We just popped around to see if you were OK, and you are, so we'll be off now, see you later, bye." As I was bundling my girlfriend out of the door, she said, "Eeeee, your mother's a bit of a queer bugger isn't she?" I said, "Oh aye, she thought I was her other son!" I don't think she believed me though.

I never did get a shag with that girl.

# Comedy inspirations

I have always let it be known that my main inspiration in comedy has been Ken Dodd. He is the master of his craft, and now, in his 80's, he is still working hard and still making people laugh. However, over the years, you meet great comedians, who just never get the big break they deserve. One of those was a guy from the North East called Johnny Hammond. I thought he was a great comedian, and would try to get to watch him work as much as possible. In fact I would go so far as to say he was a bit of a hero to me, but more than that, we became firm friends.

Eventually, Johnny decided to cut his workload down, and semi-retire. He bought a house in Southport, and enjoyed his life over there with his wife. But, he was always on the phone to me, and insisted that when I worked in the area, I must call in to see him for a cuppa. He loved chatting about the club days, and the business in general. He was so upset when I developed throat cancer, and was always there for me. He couldn't understand how I could go on stage and make jokes about it, but, as I explained to him, it was just my way of coping with it.

Johnny had a thousand stories about me, but his favourite was the time I hit a bloke with a mic stand. He would tell this story to anyone who would listen. He would be in stitches when he said, "When I asked you why you did it, you said, nobody calls my mother a cunt.............except my father."

He was a character, and he always pleaded poverty. One night, I was appearing at the Southport Theatre, and as we had sold out, the theatre manager came to the dressing room, and gave me a bottle of Champagne to celebrate. I decided that Johnny should have it, as things were getting a bit tough for him. I thought it would be a treat, and would cheer him up. After the show, I dropped it off at his house. He was so moved, and thanked me so much. Then, the bastard sold it! That was just typical of him, and it did make me laugh when I found out.

A few years earlier, when he was working, I got a phone call from him. He was due to work at Peterlee Working Men's Club, but he didn't feel well, and didn't feel like doing it, so would I do it in his place. I said that I wasn't sure, because they had booked him. He was a big name in the clubs, and had been in the Grand Final of New Faces. They wanted him, not me. He then said, "Ohh, come on Roy, you're better than nothing!" So that filled me full of confidence. Anyway, I agreed, and went to the club. I got changed in the Gents' toilet (complete with piss on the floor) and was ready to go on. That night I was introduced on stage as "Chubby Hammond." I kept the "fucks" to a minimum, and I think I got away with it.

# *Coincidence*

I mentioned in my previous book that my mother was one of five sisters and three brothers. When I was young, we lived at 78 Broadway in Grangetown, and one of my Aunties lived next door at number 80. In those days, people didn't move far away from where they were born, so it was quite common for extended families to live very close to one another. Auntie Alice was the musical one of the family, and played piano in the local club. She was brilliant, and I admired her playing skills. She could play anything, as long as she had the sheet music. In fact, it's a good job that the pigeons from the nearby pigeon lofts didn't get into the club, because if they had, they might have shit on the sheet music, and she would have played it!

When I look back now, I have to smile to myself, because I have all these fond memories of Auntie Alice, and all these years later, I became famous for a song called "Living Next Door to Alice!" Although I don't think she would have approved of the version that I am famous for.

It was around this time that a new pub opened nearby. I was still a virgin, (well, I was, but my right hand wasn't). The Magnet Hotel used to put live bands on, and was a magnet for the local girls. I still remember some of the bands. There was "Rufus Buck," "Great British Invention" and "The Freelanders." My mates and me were too young to get in, so we would just sit on the wall and watch the girls, with their short skirts and bouffant hairdos. When they had all gone in, we would listen to the bands from outside. I would always be tapping away to the music with my hands and the lads often said that I should be a drummer. They were right, and years later I regularly played drums at

The Magnet with my band. You could say that it was just a coincidence, but I sometimes think that your life is mapped out for you.

# The Band Box

I don't know if this was just a "North East" thing, but the pubs and clubs would put on what was called a "Band Box" at lunchtimes to get people in. This was well before Karaoke, and basically, anyone could get up and sing with the musicians. I used to play drums at one of these places with a woman called Doris at the piano. I loved doing these gigs, because you met so many weird and wonderful characters, and we gave them all nicknames. There was a lad we called "Sexless" because he only came once a week. Then there was "Two Pint Doris" who wouldn't sing until she'd had four halves of lager. "No Fags Dennis" was always bumming cigarettes off everyone. I also remember someone we called "Bubbles" and another called "Bucket Johnny" who was the window cleaner. He would come in, sing a song and then go back outside and clean the pub windows. There was "Tommy Rags" from the market and a guy called "Wimoweh" because he only ever sang one song, "Wimoweh!" But one of the funniest was a woman who had badly-fitting false teeth. When she talked or sang, they made a whistling sound, which was funny enough. But when she was singing, and her top set flew out of her mouth, we nearly died laughing. She'd just sung, "How Much is that Doggy in the Window" when the dentures made their break for freedom, and quick as a flash someone sang back, "Was it the one with no teeth!" I mean, you try playing on after that had happened.

These were great days and pubs were thriving. Entertainment seemed to be the key to pulling the punters in. I was talking to my driver, Keith, about this the other day. He used to sing and compere at these Band Box gigs and was telling me about when they introduced bingo at them. We all know how serious women can be when the bingo is on, so that makes what happened even funnier. People would bring their own sandwiches and pies to the pub and eat them whilst they were having a drink. On this occasion, one woman was eating a corned beef sandwich whilst also marking her bingo card. As she took a bite, some of it must have gone down the wrong way. She started to choke, but the caller just carried on. He never flinched as he said, "On its own, number four. Two and six, twenty-six. If you're going to baulk pet, could you go into the passageway. Seven and five, seventy-five. Three and two, thirty-two." That is how serious they took their bingo around our way.

# *My First Groupie*

B ack in 1972, the band was just starting to take off, and we were getting regular work. Our agent would often call us with last minute bookings, and this was one of those times. The gig was at a club in a place called Brough, on the A66, near a village called Kirkby Stephen.

Agents were always trying to protect their business, and they were always frightened of losing the club for future bookings, so we always got a pep talk from them before the gigs. This was no exception, "This is only a small club," he said. "Remember to keep the volume down, and be on your best behaviour, as you are representing my agency."

After everyone had been picked up, we set off in our Thames 15cwt van, a right, rickety piece of shit, if you've ever seen one! But it did get us to most of our gigs on time, and it was all that we could afford. Once again, to everyone's surprise, we arrived at the venue on time, and went into the concert room. I couldn't help noticing the short, dumpy barmaid. She was definitely giving me the eye, but I just carried on setting the gear up.

When we were all happy with the sound etc. I headed off to the bar, bought a drink, and got a wink. After that, the drinks came free, usually accompanied by suggestive comments. So, whilst the bingo was on, and the bar was quiet, I decided to have a chat with her. She told me that there was a great nightclub in Penrith, and she would be going there after work. She asked if I'd like to go with her. Sadly, I had to explain that as we all travelled together in the van I couldn't go with her, as I would be without a lift home. She looked a bit disappointed, but seemed to accept it.

In those days, closing time in the clubs was 10.30pm, so at 10.45pm we were at the bottom of the fire escape with our gear. I was dying for a piss, due to the 6 large bottles of Newcastle Brown Ale I'd consumed. So, I was just about to use the "Artistes Private Toilet Facilities," or the wall at the back of the club as it was also known, when Miss Dumpy groped me from behind. At this point, I have to say that, when God handed out pricks, I thought he meant we were being immunised against some sort of disease, and as I'm afraid of needles, I asked for a small one! She spun me around, and started to kiss me. She took me totally by surprise, and her lips were like a sink plunger. It felt like all that I had eaten that day was being sucked out of my stomach. Then, she dragged me against the dustbins and had my cock in her mouth before I could blink. She was quicker than a rat up a drainpipe. As she pushed me to the floor, I could hear all the lads laughing. I had been taken completely by surprise, and was now totally at her mercy. In a blind panic, I shouted at them, "Does anyone want to fuck this?" to which came the reply, "Piss off, we don't want sloppy seconds" followed by more laughter. It took a couple of days for me to laugh about this incident, and the lads in the band never let me forget it. To make things worse, all I could think of was the agent laying down the law and telling US to behave! - Remember, there's no such thing as a "free drink!"

# The Diet Club

As the band became more successful, I have to admit that it went to my head a bit. I really believed that as the drummer in a band, I was a bit of a heartthrob, and that I could pull any bird I wanted. However, I was getting aware that I should try to lose a bit of weight. So, along with my mate, Marty, I joined a well-known diet club. You can imagine what it was like when we turned up for our first meeting at The Memorial Hall in Redcar. The room was full of larger ladies, and we were the only men there, but we were determined to give this our best shot. We were weighed, given our exercise and diet sheets, and off we went.

The following week, we arrived for the "weigh-in," and stood at the back of the room, out of the way. There was absolutely no way that I was going to stand near the middle of the floor, just in case the combined weight of all those fatties was too much for it to take. I mean, every one of them was built like a small dumper truck! The class started with the class leader welcoming everyone and giving her morale-building speech. We kept a low profile at the back, but when she had finished, she asked everyone to turn around. You've guessed it, the scales were at the back of the room, so when everyone turned around, we were at the front.

As the weigh-in started, she called out names. When your name was called, you had to go up in front of everybody, get weighed, and she would then tell the class how much weight you had lost. The whole group would then applaud you. But, if you hadn't lost anything, or worse still, gained weight, you had to explain why, to the group. As we were the only men, Marty and I stood out like a sausage roll at a Bar Mitzvah.

My turn came, and I was called up to the scales. She looked at them; looked in her book, looked back at them, looked at me, then addressed the room. "Ladies, Mr. Vasey has put on two pounds." She looked at me and asked for an explanation. I felt like a naughty schoolboy. Quick as a flash, I said, "Well you're not going to believe this, but I was walking past the cake shop, when this custard slice jumped out and got me in a headlock. Bugger me, as I managed to break free, I was tripped up by a box of biscuits – chocolate ones, would you believe." Everyone laughed, and I think I got away with it. We had many more weeks like that, and my excuses became the highlight of the meetings.  Oh happy days.

I've always carried weight, and I've always tried to keep a lid on it, but being on the road so much, means eating the wrong things at the wrong times. So, the long "Summer Seasons" in Blackpool allowed me to try to keep my weight down. One particular year, I decided to go to Slimming World in Blackpool as a private client. I mentioned this to Pete Richardson and Steve Cowper who were both working with me at the time, and to be honest, were both a little on the chunky side. As it's always easier to stick to a diet if a few of you do it together, I asked them if they wanted to come with me. They agreed, and we had a few drinks and an "Indian" as a last supper. At the meal, I said that as an incentive, I would give the lads £10 for every one pound lost in the first week. They were delighted with the offer, and couldn't wait to get started.

The next day, we all went off to see Maggie, who was the Slimming World lady. We got weighed, and took our diet sheets and instructions away. I stuck to the new diet regime religiously, and was really pleased with my progress through the week. I knew that Pete and Steve liked a drink and a kebab, so I knew that my money was safe.

The week flew by, and it was time to see Maggie. I got weighed first, and had lost four pounds. The lads gave me a sarcastic round of applause, and a few comments about not trying very hard. Steve then got on the scales, and had lost an amazing eight pounds! Pete clapped, and said, "Well done Steve." He then looked at me and said, "Go on Roy, pay the man." I was now £80 lighter. Then Pete approached the scales. He looked at me, and then stood on them. Maggie looked at the scales, looked back up at Pete, and asked him to get off. She then reset them and asked him to get back on. She looked at the dial again, put her specs on, checked once more, and said; "I have never seen anyone lose this much in a week...........EVER!" He had lost SEVENTEEN pounds. Pete just smiled and held his hand out. "£170 for me, I think." I couldn't believe it. I asked Maggie if she was in on a joke, but she wasn't. He really had lost seventeen pounds. I paid up, and congratulated him. I didn't know how he'd done it, but the scales didn't lie.

When we were going through the stories for this book, I talked to Pete about this incident, and asked him how he had managed it. He laughed, and said, "Do you really want to know?" I said "Yes, and I'm not going to ask for my money back, so you can tell the truth." Now I'm not saying Pete is a sneaky bastard, but.... He told me that after the "Indian" the night before that first meeting, he had been for a kebab and a few more pints. Then, in the morning, he had eaten a full English breakfast and drunk about four pints of water. He had been desperate to go to the toilet, but had managed to hold it all in until he had been weighed. The following week, he hadn't eaten anything the day before, or on the morning of the weigh in. He had also made sure he had been to the toilet, was wearing less clothing than the previous week and hadn't got any loose change in his pocket. On reflection, he is a sneaky bastard.

We all lost quite a bit of weight over the next couple of months. In fact my belly started to disappear and my stage suits became too big for me. I even featured in a magazine article about how I managed to lose weight. There was now a bit of a problem, because I was known as "Chubby" and now I wasn't! Maggie came up with an idea. She was a seamstress, and made clothes, curtains etc. Her idea was to make me a "Fat Body Suit" that I could wear underneath my shirt. It did the trick, and I used it for quite a while until I put the weight back on and was back to being a real "Chubby" again.

A few years later, a new TV show was aired, called "Fat Club." It was a programme where members of the public were put through a weight loss programme of diet and exercise. They had an army physical training instructor to put them through their paces, and shout a lot! The series proved popular and was a big hit. After a couple of series, they came up with the idea of making a celebrity version of the show. Unfortunately, no celebs would go on a show called "Fat Club," so they had to change the name to "Celebrity Fit Club," and guess who they wanted to appear on it, me! George told me about their enquiry, but we agreed that I wouldn't do it; I needed to keep on the chubbier side. Oh well, their loss was my (weight) gain!

# Chips, A Tactless Man

When I worked with The Four Man Band, we used to love playing at Eston Club and Institute. One evening, I called at the club, as I had to see the committee about something. Johnny Hammond was stood at the bar, so I joined him. The club was holding a charity fund-raising event that night, and several acts had agreed to appear, free of charge, to help the cause. The host for the evening was a local "character" who, for some unknown reason was called "Chips." As I looked at the stage, he was up there doing his bit. He was one of those people who would do anything for charity, and, of course, it was nothing to do with the fact that he got free booze for doing these shows.

"Chips" was not known for being tactful, and this night he took his lack of tact to new levels. He stood on that stage and said, "Ladies and Gentlemen, we are here tonight to raise money for these unfortunate people in wheelchairs, because they are not like us. They can't run for a bus, they can't play football or jump over a fence." Talk about tactless, Johnny and I were cringing and wanted a big hole to open up in the floor, so we could climb in and hide. It couldn't possibly get any worse could it? Well, yes it could, because he carried on by saying, "Would the head cripple come up onstage and accept this cheque." You couldn't make it up! Johnny and I just had to leave, we didn't know whether to laugh or cry.

# Phone Box or Public Convenience

When I was in the band with George Proudman and Mick Boothby, we would have lots of fun. We were like a family because we spent so much time together. One night, we were travelling home from a gig when the van broke down. George and I decided to walk back to a phone box that we had passed about a mile back and Mick stayed with the van. George was going to ring a mate who could come and tow us home.

It took us about 20 minutes to reach the phone box, and by that time I was bursting for a piss. So, as George made the call, I relieved myself against the side of the phone box. Isn't it strange how us blokes need something to piss against! Anyway, I noticed that the inside of the phone box was steaming up, and as it happened, George didn't look too pleased. You see, the glass panes at the bottom of the box had been smashed and I was pissing straight into it, and all over George's trousers. To say he wasn't best pleased was a bit of an understatement. I just laughed and explained that when you've got to go, you've got to go. George had no choice but to carry on with the phone call and get us some help. But with the strong smell of Sugar Puffs in the phone box, he was quickly done. He chased me all the way back to the van, and we still laugh about this incident. Well I still do, I don't know about George.

# Comedy in the Blood

They say that comedy is in the blood and on the whole, I agree, but there have been many times when I wasn't so sure. Every comedian has bad nights, and I've had my fair share. Throughout the early days, I often felt like giving up and getting a proper job. At least that way you would get paid each week for doing your job, instead of some jumped-up little Hitler telling you that you were shite, and he wasn't going to pay you. There would be many days when I'd be sitting in my little flat above the hairdresser's shop with only a quarter of a pint of milk that had gone a bit off, a half eaten biscuit and a tea bag that had been used more times than Jordan's dildo! I would be so depressed, and I couldn't even turn to my parents, because my father "liked a drink," and my mother just liked to moan at everything. I've lost count of the number of times I've seen my father's hands around my mother's throat, nowadays they would have been the perfect guests on "The Jeremy Kyle Show." Eventually, my mother left, and my father brought me up.

Between them, they had no parenting skills, and I was pretty much left to my own devices. It was just a normal way of life to me, but I was sure there was something out there better than what I had. I ran wild, and considered myself a bit of a bad lad, and at 12 years old, my weapon of choice was a stick! In fact, it was the stick that used to keep the next-door neighbour's peas and beans up straight until I stole it. I'm not asking for sympathy, but I can't ever remember having a breakfast when I was young. I just remember that if you walked up to the end of the street, you could smell the bacon and eggs cooking at Laney's Café. I know this sounds like the Monty Python sketch, but me and my mates would go down to Dorman Long steelworks, where we would climb over the fence and sneak into where they put the big ingots (from the furnaces at the steel mill) to cool. That was where we kept warm for the day. To us, this was much better than being in school, so that's why we bunked off to go there. My mother wasn't bothered where I was during the day, so long as I wasn't at home. I never realised that this was because my dad's best mate was "giving her one" over the kitchen sink.

I did love my mother, and once bought her a box of chocolates. She was over the moon. I suppose that because my dad never bought her anything, this was quite a big deal for her. She thanked me, and said, "You're a good lad." What she didn't know was that I had nicked the money out of her purse to buy them. I don't know if she ever found that out, but if she did, she never said anything to me.

Despite everything, I always had the ability to make my mum and dad laugh. I was a cheeky little git, and had an answer for everything. If I left anything on my plate, dad would come out with the usual parental line that there were kids in Africa starving and running about with no shoes on their feet. I would just say, "Well, they can have mine if they want." He used to say to my mother, "He's so sharp, he should watch he doesn't cut himself with that tongue of his!"

I had posters on my bedroom wall, and amongst them were Tommy Steele and Marty Wilde, who were big stars at the time. When the posters went up around town advertising that they were coming to Middlesbrough Town Hall, I asked my dad if I could go and see them. His reply was, "The only stars you'll be seeing is when I bash you over your fucking head, now bugger off and go and tidy your room up."

I suppose what I am saying is that I think that growing up this way has made me what I am. I had a tough start in life, so I became tough. But I found humour in everything, which I now know was a coping mechanism. Despite all this, I really do believe that comedy is in my blood. Even the bad things that have happened to me over the years have shaped what I have achieved, and that includes my act.

If I had to offer any advice to young comedians who are just starting out, it would be use your life experiences and write something new and fresh every day. Don't go into comedy thinking about the money aspect, because only a few actually make it big. Remember, you are not going to get laughs at every gig, but with time, you will improve and the bad nights will become fewer. As you write your material, try it out on friends and family. I tried my stuff out on the public when I worked on the market. I can't believe the crap that I got away with!

Back in those days, I was always chasing the girls and would tell gags to try and get off with them. Most girls wouldn't give you a second look if you didn't have a car. There was no way you could pull a girl if she had to ride home on the crossbar of your bike, but I did managed to get my fair share by making them laugh. Pulling a bird was tough back then, I mean now, if you want to get a shag in Blackpool during the lights, you just need to be in possession of two arms, two legs and a dick. I think I was born too early!

When I look back, I suppose I've always been fascinated with show business. As a kid, if I saw someone on a poster or with his or her name in lights, I assumed that they would be millionaires, and have a house in Hollywood. Well, now I'm on those posters, and have my name outside theatres, and I can tell you it's not like that. OK, I have made a fair amount of money and done quite well for myself, but I thought I'd made it when I bought a flat in Scarborough.

I am a bit of a "one off" in the entertainment world, and I am quite aware that some people don't like what I do. I have lots of good friends within the business, but I also know that some entertainers hate me, even though they have never met me. One person in particular really annoyed me, and that was the comedian, Lennie Bennett. The first time that I met him was at a charity cricket match in Blackpool. All the stars from the Summer Shows were there, and many of them had their own prime time TV shows. Most of them were happy for me to be there, and we were all getting along fine. Then I saw Lennie Bennett, who was hosting a TV game show at the time. I went over to say hello, and put my hand out to shake hands with him and he just turned away and completely ignored me. What a Tosser! I have to be honest, it did upset me at the time, but a few days later, I was talking to Bernard Manning and told him the story. He told me that he thought that Lennie Bennett was a complete prat who had a face like a smacked arse. He thought he was the unfunniest man in Britain. On top of that, nobody in show business liked him. In fact when he died, I don't think anyone from our business turned up at his funeral, which I suppose is a bit sad, but what do you expect if you treat people the way he did me.

Another time that I felt really upset was when I recorded "Living Next Door to Alice." It became a massive hit, and I achieved a lifetime ambition by appearing on Top of The Pops." When I did the song in my live shows, the audience went mad, singing along at the top of their voices. I felt like a pop star, it was a great time in my career. We were due to record the next live DVD, and intended to include "Alice," so we had to get permission from the writers of the song. They now live in Los Angeles, so my office approached them for permission. They refused point blank to allow it. Apparently, they didn't want to be associated with me, they didn't like me, or my act. I took it very personally, as they had made a judgment about me, when they didn't even know me, and that's what hurts. They didn't seem that bothered when they happily took the royalties from the chart success of the single!

I have had similar treatment from club acts in the past, and one time many years ago, when I opened my act with a Tony Christie song, I fell foul of the other act on the bill. I had finished my act and returned to the dressing room. He charged in and had a right go at me. He didn't like me, or my act, and accused me of stealing one of his best songs. I pointed out that it wasn't one of his best songs; it was one of Tony Christie's best songs. He didn't like that and called me "A Big Fat, Pig Faced Cunt." I have been called some things in my time, but a Big, Fat, Pig-Faced Cunt was a new one to me. After about five minutes of this abuse, I politely told him that he was an "Ugly, Rat-Faced, Fucking TWAT." I think the whole club heard him scream like a girl as I grabbed him by his throat and suggested that he didn't talk to me like that again. As I loosened my grip, he turned and ran out of the club leaving his speaker system, which obviously wasn't very good, because I didn't get very much for it when I sold it!

Those were the days of what was known as "Pro–Digs." These were B&B's that specialised in showbiz acts. There were so many clubs in the UK, that entertainers were travelling the length and breadth of the country working. Normal B&B's would lock the doors at 10.00pm, so they were no use to us. Pro-Digs were used to us all arriving late with our cans of beer, bottles of Vodka etc. so we could wind down with a drink and a good laugh. We would talk about our gigs and the clubs where we were all working. It was sort of like an Alcoholics or Gamblers Anonymous meeting for entertainers, but we drank like fishes, and gambled our earnings away.

One night, a girl singer called "Christine" arrived late. It was either her time of the month, or she had just had a very bad gig. She flung the door open, stormed in and poured a large red wine. "Fuck 'em" she said. "Fuck the Club, Fuck that Concert Secretary, Fuck the Band, in fact, Fuck everyone!" I turned around just in time to see a comedian friend of mine taking his clothes off. I said, "What are you doing?" to which he replied, "If she's going to Fuck everyone, I want to be in there first." Everyone burst out laughing, including Christine. You see, we all knew how she felt, and with one action like that, she was back in the real world with her work mates. We all supported each other, and we always had a good laugh.

In the early 1980's TV started to kill comedians because there was such a demand for them on TV that they couldn't keep up with new material. The TV comedians were now getting a bit expensive for the clubs, and they were looking for new talent. At the time, I was doing a routine about the adverts on TV, which was working really well. I performed this routine at a "Shop Window" which is a show put on by the agents for the club bookers. After the show, I was approached by an agent who wanted to put me in for a five-day run at the Hacienda Club in Tyneside. I jumped at the chance, as it was quite good money for me. The time came, and I arrived at the club to do my show. Well, I died on my arse every single one of those five nights. This was one of those times that I was seriously thinking of packing it all in. Anyway, I went to see the agent, and got the shock of my life when he gave me my wages in full. I couldn't believe it, and told him that I'd died a death every night. I really didn't think I'd get my full money, but he explained. "I knew you wouldn't do well, they don't like comedians and nobody gets laughs there." I didn't understand, and asked why he had put me in there then. "Well" he said, "they owe me money, so I was just trying to get my own back. Don't worry about it, it's a shit club and is just a "knocking shop" where the lads go for a bit of pussy, and the girls go for a bit of dick. Nobody is bothered about the acts, just forget it and enjoy the money."

Life is full of bullshit and the older you get, the more of it you see and do, but for me, I started very young. As I mentioned, my mother abandoned me when I was just a kid, so I would live off other people's sympathies. There's no wonder that I took the route in life that I did; it was purely about survival. I had no real guidance, but when the Police surrounded our house at eight o'clock in the morning, I definitely knew I'd done something wrong. I've been on probation more times than Ronald Biggs. But, throughout these times, I would always be writing down jokes and poems that I had made up. I had no idea that one day I would get into show business. I would tell jokes to friends, but I didn't know how they would react. Sometimes they laughed, other times they would just talk over the joke and change the subject, which upset me, but made me try harder the next time.

Eventually, the "Chubby" character was born. He came out of the comedy duo, "Allcock and Brown," hence the flying helmet. I once was asked if I wore the flying helmet because I was bald. Well, strangely enough, my father was bald, my Uncle Ted was bald, and Uncle Arthur was bald. It's a wonder my fucking mother wasn't bald! There's nothing wrong with being bald, but let's be honest, if you had a bald dog, you wouldn't want to pat it would you? Whilst we're on the subject of dogs, I've buried three of them in my lifetime, but two of them were just asleep! Anyway, I might be losing my hair now, but back then I had a fine head of hair. My dad used to say that being bald was supposed to be sexy; Kojak was a big hit on the telly at that time. I told him that Kojak shaved his head to take the attention away from his ugly face!

Whilst I was living in a flat at 54 Corporation Road in Redcar, I had time on my hands, so I became a frequent visitor to Walker's Saleroom. I had been watching Top of the Pops, and seen Gilbert O'Sullivan. He was playing an upright piano, and seemed to be creating the rhythm by using one finger on the bass notes. I had always fancied learning to play the piano, and after seeing this, I thought that I could give it a go. So, when a piano came up at the saleroom, I bought it for £5.00. I then rang a few mates to help me get it into the flat. We were like that Laurel and Hardy film where they tried to get the piano up the steep steps, but eventually got it into my flat.

The piano became my pride and joy and I practiced night and day. I actually felt a bit sorry for Tim who lived in the flat below me, I mean, I was really bad. After about a year, I bumped into him in the hallway and he surprised me by saying that my playing had improved so much. That little comment gave me so much pleasure and I invited him up for a cup of tea. I then started playing the piano whilst he watched. He said, "I've noticed that you're not playing the black notes." I said, "I know, I'm prejudiced!" He asked what key I was playing in, "Yale" was my flippant reply.

I was divorced by then, and had my two boys, Richard and Robert. They would come to see me at the flat on a Saturday. We would play ball on the grass outside and go down to the beach for an ice cream. I enjoyed having them, but it was a bit of a sad time in my life, because I wasn't there for them when they needed me. I was a "Saturday Dad" and looking back, I feel bad about neglecting them as they grew up. I was more interested about becoming a successful comedian.

I also neglected my relationships with women, my work was more important to me. I remember one girlfriend who became obsessed with spying on me. She was convinced that I must have been seeing other women, when I was actually working. She even took to parking up across the road and spying at me through two holes cut in a newspaper. She would have made a dreadful spy. One day, she told me she was pregnant and that I might be the father. Nowadays, finding out if you are the father of a baby is easy, you just go on Jeremy Kyle, but in those days you had to have a blood test, which could only prove that you weren't the father. So I said to her that as far as I knew, I wasn't her only boyfriend and that I knew she had slept around a bit. She stormed off, and I never saw her again. I don't know if she had a boy or a girl, but that child will be grown up by now and possibly have children. I never found out if I was its father, maybe one day I'll get a knock on the door. Maybe it wasn't mine, I guess I'll never really know.

I had some great years playing in bands, but all good things come to an end. I had ended up as the comedy drummer in a cabaret-type group. We were a bit like "The Black Abbotts" and "The Grumblweeds," but people left the band and we ended up as the comedy duo, "Allcock and Brown." I, of course have never been All Cock, so I had to be Brown. This is where the flying hat came from. Eventually, I became a solo act, and had to earn my living in the pubs and clubs of the North East. It wasn't easy, but it did give me a great apprenticeship. I, along with all the other acts would work our guts out, but the audiences could be very difficult to please. It wasn't just the audiences either; the Concert Secretaries could be right bastards too.

# The Vicar Incident

Allcock and Brown were performing at The Ranch House Club in the North East.

We were on stage, and having a great show. At that time, we were doing silly impressions and risqué routines. The audiences seemed to like what we were doing, and our bookings were looking good. On this particular night, the club was full, and we were about to do a comedy routine where I dressed up as a vicar and complained about the act. To make it work, I needed to come from the back of the club, so I came off the side of the stage and quickly changed into my vicar's outfit. Then I went out of the back door and ran around to the front of the club. I had done this hundreds of times before. But this time, I came across the doorman with a conscience.

I stood in the doorway and got into my "vicar character," but as I approached the door to the concert room, the doorman stopped me. He said, "I'm sorry vicar, but you can't go in there, there's a rude act on, and it's not suitable for you." I tried to explain who I was, but he wouldn't believe me. He thought that I really was a vicar, and I was trying to get into the room to see what was going on. He thought that I might make a complaint about the type of acts that the club was putting on, and he wasn't going to allow that. The more I protested, the more stubborn he became, but I needed to get in, as my part was coming up. Eventually, there was only one thing for it. I said, "Listen, if you don't let me in right now, I'll kick you right in the fucking bollocks!" He looked shocked, and I think that that was the point in the conversation where he realised that I wasn't a real vicar. I pushed my way into the concert room just in time to shout out, "This act is disgusting, I wish to make a complaint." The poor doorman didn't know whether to laugh or cry, but he did see the funny side of what had happened.

Don't Kick me in the Bollocks

THE DOORMAN AT RANCHOUSE,

# No Second Spot

I was always short of cash, and looked forward to doing gigs to get paid and be able to pay the rent and buy food. One particular night, I was booked to appear at Peterlee Social Club and on my arrival I sought out the Concert Chairman, who turned out to be yet another Little Hitler. I said, "Hello mate, I'm the comedian for tonight." His reply to this was, "It's not mate, it's Mr. Chairman to you! You'll be on at half past eight for your first spot. I don't want any blue stuff, no swearing, keep it clean. Then it'll be the bingo, and you will do your second spot at 9.30."

I did my first spot, and kept it clean as requested. I seemed to go down quite well and I returned to the dressing room. Hitler followed me in and I said to him, "Was that OK for you Mr. Chairman?" He said, "Well there's one or two things I need to speak to you about." I immediately said, "There's nothing to worry about in my second spot, I open up with a George Formby song on the ukulele, followed by a couple of impressions from the TV and some spoofs of adverts." He said, "Can I just stop you there son, there won't be any room on the stage." I asked why, and he said, "Because there'll be another comedian stood on the stage taking your place, so if you don't mind, fuck off!"

These Concert Chairmen might have been twats, but some of them did at least manage to come up with new ways of telling you that you were crap.

# Welcome to the Club

Every act that has ever worked in "the clubs" has stories to tell, and I'm no different. I told quite a few stories in my first book, but there are loads more. I've lost count of the number of times I turned up at a club to be greeted by some jumped-up trout of a concert secretary, who treated me like dog turd on a shoe, and I was the turd!

When I look back now, I have to laugh at these guys. They book "Chubby" Brown, the filthiest man on the planet, then tell you, "I want no bad language on that stage, NO Arse, Tit, Fanny, Dick, and definitely NO CUNTS!" Well, that would have been difficult, because all the cunts were usually in the Committee Room, having a fucking meeting.

It wasn't just the concert secretaries; the doormen were a breed unto themselves too. When I refer to doormen, I don't mean a big bruiser in a dinner suit and bow tie. These guys were often older men, who usually had a Woodbine cigarette hanging from their mouths, and an attitude to match. To give you an idea of what they could be like, I arrived at the front door of a club one night to be greeted by the doorman. I was carrying my props for the show; I had half a table tennis bat under one arm, a plastic dog, a tennis racket, a polystyrene bog door, a talking bucket and a mop. The doorman took one look at me and said, "Who are you?" so after biting my tongue I said, "I'm the act." He looked at his signing-in book then back at me, and said, "You'll have to sign in before I can let you through." By now my patience was wearing thin, but I thought that I'd better be polite, as I really needed the money that night. I asked if I could go and put my stuff in the dressing room before I dropped it all, and then come back to sign in. "No, you're not allowed in the Concert Room unless you've signed in, and to get to the dressing room, you have to walk through the Concert Room!" He was in charge of that door, and he was there to enforce the rules. I just looked at him and finally lost it. "What do you want me to do, shall I go back to the car and get a cabbage, then we can have a game of Cabbages and Kings from fucking Crackerjack, you thick arsehole!" He just looked at me, and then he looked back at the book. So, I put the stuff down, and signed in. You couldn't win with these guys.

They weren't all like that; some of them could be almost human. When I was a young, fresh-faced comedian in 1972 and working for Brian Findlay's agency, they sent me to Seaton Carew Caravan Club on a wet and windy November night. The Caravan Park had closed for the season, but the clubhouse was still open. I arrived at the front door (with my props) to be greeted by the doorman. This was one of the nicer ones, and he welcomed me to the club. It was freezing, and I wondered how many people would turn up on a night like that. He quickly answered that question, "We've only sold two tickets," he said, "I don't understand why they haven't cancelled the show." One of the ticket holders was stood at the bar and he looked like a right miserable bastard, so I said, "Should I just put the stuff back in the car and fuck off home?" The doorman thought it was probably for the best. So, I put the stuff back in the car, and when I'd finished, he called me over. To my surprise, he offered to pay me "a couple of bob" for my trouble. He held his hand out, with some cash in it, but before he let go, he said, "Before you go, could you wait until the other guy turns up with his ticket, then you can explain it all to him." I had travelled to the club to *not* do my job, and ended up doing the fucking doorman's job!

# The Organ

The Mineworkers Club was just a few miles south of Sunderland and it was the scene of what has become known as, "The Organ Story." It was a notoriously tough club to work, but I didn't let that bother me. I was full of confidence, and thought that I could tame this crowd. How wrong was I?

I did my first spot, and to be honest, I did struggle. I retired to the safety of the dressing room, and was working out what I could do in my second spot to win them round and I became aware that the break seemed longer than normal. The Concert Secretary then came into the room. "Oh, you're still here?" he said. I reminded him that I still had a second spot to do, and he just laughed. He informed me that they'd had a quick meeting of the committee and decided that I was crap, so they didn't want me for my second spot. Not only that, but they had decided that they weren't going to pay me, and that included my expenses. You could say that I wasn't very happy about this, and I wasn't going to take it lying down.

Whilst all this was going on, I could hear the organ playing in the club, which was quite normal. They had told me earlier in the evening that this was a brand new organ that they were thinking of buying, and that tonight a professional organist would be playing it as a demonstration. They told me how much it was going to cost them and I do remember thinking that it was a substantial amount of money. I immediately hatched a plan.

I waited for a break in the performance and as it came, I marched out on to the stage and grabbed the microphone. Everyone in the room looked at me as I began to speak. I appealed to their sense of fair play, and said that I thought that it was unfair that I had travelled there and done a spot, and had been told that I wasn't being paid. I thought that wrong and they should at least cover my expenses. Unfortunately, they all seemed to agree with the committee and I was hit by what seemed like a thousand beer mats. I saw red, and stormed across the stage to the organ. Somehow, I summoned up the strength and picked up one end of the organ, which had the bench seat attached to it. The organist slid off the bench and straight into a couple of tables full of drinks. Then, when I got my arms around it I lifted it off the ground.

As I stood there holding the organ, I shouted at the concert secretary that I wanted my full fee of £75, and that if they didn't give it to me, the organ would get dropped. This seemed to do the trick, and he waved the £75 in his hand whilst pleading with me not to hurt the organ. I told him that no harm would come to the organ if they did as they were told. I certainly wasn't going to lose my bargaining tool, so I told him to come over to me and put the money into my pocket. Slowly, he moved forward, and carefully placed the cash in my pocket. I had won, the money was in my possession, and I had been paid. Then, the Treasurer approached me and held out his payments book. "You'll have to sign for your money," he said. Without thinking, I gently put the organ down and took the book and pen from him. As I signed my name, several large miners, jumped me. They beat seven bells of shit out of me whilst the Concert Secretary removed the £75 from my pocket. I was then unceremoniously dumped in a heap outside the back doors of the club. The next day, to add insult to injury, I got a phone call from my agent, Brian Findlay, to tell me that the club had been on the phone and told him that they were not satisfied with the quality of my performance, and would not be paying me and wouldn't entertain a return booking within the near future! I wish that I had dropped that fucking organ now.

# The Wrong Gig

Sometimes you can be booked for the wrong gig. That happened to me when I was booked to appear at The Ladle Hotel in the North East. I was told that it was a "Special" evening. As usual, I turned up with my props, and went to the dressing room to get ready. I knew that the audience was having a meal, followed by the entertainment, but that really was all I knew. As I sat in the dressing room, I could hear the faint sound of "posh music" as I called it, but I didn't think anything about it.

The dressing room door opened, in walked my mate and comedy hero, Johnny Hammond. He had been working at a nearby club, and decided to call in to see me. Unfortunately, he didn't have time to warn me what he had seen as he came into the venue, because the compere followed him into the room. He had come in to make sure that I was ready to go on stage, and as they were on to the cheese and biscuits, it would be quite soon. I looked at Johnny, and said, "This sounds like a classy do." The compere then said, "Oh yes, it is classy, and they're all looking forward to a great night and some nice clean comedy." Well, I was always being told that I had to be clean; people said it to wind me up. Little did I know, this wasn't a wind-up. As I stood waiting to go on, he started the evening off by saying, "My Lords, Ladies and Gentlemen, Lord Mayor and Lady Mayoress, Chief Constable and Mrs............" My heart sank, but it was too late now. Apparently, the event was to celebrate the engagement of the Mayor's son to the Chief Constable's daughter. All the local dignitaries were in attendance, and I was the first act on. I was introduced, and bounded on to the stage. My usual opening line was, "Good evening, I'm "Chubby" Brown, my wife's got two cunts, and I'm one of them!" but I thought that might be a bit strong with this audience, so I said "Did you hear about the Siamese twins who were joined at the nose, the first words they said to one another was, who the fuck are you looking at!" That was always a sure-fire winner of a gag, but not this time. The room was silent except for a few nervous coughs. I carried on with a few more of my best gags, and it wasn't getting any better. Suddenly a woman in a ball gown and tiara stood up and shouted, "how much longer are we going to put up with this filth?" The woman next to her banged the table and shouted, "Here, Here!" I looked over and came out with one of my best ad-libs. "What's up with Minge and Bracket over there?" Needless to say I had to leave the stage and didn't get paid.

Back in the dressing room, I met up with Johnny Hammond. I was feeling really down and poured out my heart to him. I told him that this was the fourth gig this week where I hadn't been paid. My wife was really going to give me such a hard time. He looked at me and offered his commiserations, then he said, "Hang on a minute, it's only Tuesday, and you've not been paid for four gigs, how's that happened?" I told him that I'd been thrown out of St. Peter's Catholic Club on Saturday evening, The Stockton-on-Tees Ladies' Bowling, Knitting and Whist Drive on Sunday lunch and Our Holy Mother of Jerusalem Tabernacle last night. Johnny suggested that I changed my agent to someone who wasn't religious, that way I might end up doing the Dockers' Club or The Reprieved Murderers' Social Club in some far away place like Baghdad. It had to be better than all these Catholic Clubs in the North East. He was right, but it still took some time to be able to move on and get work more suited to my act. But I did, and the rest is history.

# *Berlin*

M y first manager was a lovely guy and a great friend.

Brian Findlay was one of the lads, he loved a drink, fag and a fuck and not necessarily in that order. He was so down to earth, that his idea of a luxury holiday was a fortnight in a caravan at Crimdon Dene. His office was so scruffy, it looked like an Al-Qaeda training camp after the American Air Force had remodelled it with a cruise missile! But he did look after me and was always looking for new gigs to do.

One day, he rang me with the news that he had secured six gigs on the trot in Berlin. I thought Berlin must be a new club that had opened, so I asked him where it was. "It's in Germany you thick cunt," he said. "But don't worry, cos I'm coming with you." I didn't know if that was a good or bad thing, but I agreed to do it.

We had to drive there, so you can imagine the fun we had trying to drive on the other side of the road. Our map-reading wasn't great and satellite navigation systems for cars didn't exist, but we managed to drive through France and Belgium and headed towards Berlin through what was known as "The Russian Corridor." You have to remember that The Berlin Wall was still up, and Russia controlled large areas of the country. The closer we got, the more apprehensive I became. Eventually, we arrived in Berlin, but immediately found ourselves lost! Brian said to me, "Go and ask that bloke over there where Montgomery Barracks is." I said, "Fuck off, you ask him. He'll be German and won't like us because we won the war!" We were both as thick as shit and thought that as soon as they realised we were English, we would get shot. We were very naïve in those days.

After about an hour of driving around and getting more and more pissed off, I snapped. "Right" I said, "I've had enough, this isn't meant to be, so let's fuck off home to England." Brian, who was also quite pissed off, agreed. So we started to look for signs to get us out of the city and back to Calais. As we turned a corner, Brian shouted out, "LOOK," there was a sign for "Montgomery Barracks," so we followed it and arrived at the barracks shortly after. We pulled up at the gatehouse and told them who we were. Soon after, we were inside meeting the people who had booked me. They made us feel so welcome, but I was still a bit apprehensive about these gigs. Brian tried to calm me down, and explained that Bob Hope used to do these sorts of gigs. There wouldn't be many in the audience, but they would really appreciate me going there for them. I could see what he was getting at, and decided that I would just try to relax and get on with my job.

The next day, at the appointed time, I was ready to go to the first gig. A sergeant told me to follow him to the transport to the gig. I was expecting a Land Rover or something similar, but I got a shock when we went outside to the helicopter. It is well known that I don't like flying, but this was really taking the piss. It was one of those helicopters that looked like a "Bubble Car" at the front. They put me in the front seat, next to the pilot, and securely strapped me in. The whole of the front of this helicopter was glass, and you could see everywhere. The pilot started the engine and we lifted off the ground. Then, the bloody thing tipped forward as we moved off. It felt like I was going to fall out and go straight through the glass window. How on earth it managed to fly with the weight of that turd in my underpants is a mystery to me.

As we flew, the pilot said to me, through the headphones, "I'll be dropping you off inside the prison." I looked at him, and said, "Prison?" He went on to tell me that we were flying in to Spandau Prison to entertain the troops who were guarding the Nazi, "Rudolf Hess," who was the only prisoner there. He had been Hitler's deputy early in the war, but had mysteriously flown to Scotland where he was arrested and held as a prisoner of war until his trial for war crimes. He was sentenced to life, and was held in Spandau until his death in 1987.

On our arrival, we were taken to a small canteen where we got talking to a Staff Sergeant who told us all about Hess, and the Nazi obsession with eliminating the Jews. Brian, who wasn't the most tactful of people, turned to me and said "You'd better not do the gags about the gas oven then!" I mean he was so tactless, he once called a one-legged man that he had just met, Stumpy! Anyway, the Sergeant asked if we would like to catch a glimpse of Hess, as he was due out in the exercise yard shortly. I thought that I should take the opportunity to see this monster of a man, as it would be something to tell my grandchildren in the future. So, we were taken to a room where we could see the exercise yard. I don't really know what I expected to see, but I didn't expect him to look like Andy Capp. He was a small elderly man and was wearing a cap and had a fag hanging from his mouth. He looked just like the cartoon character, and I couldn't imagine how this man could have once been so powerful and so feared. Brian said, "Wouldn't you just like to shoot him?" to the Sergeant, but he told us that their orders were to keep him locked up, and make sure he doesn't die. It did seem odd to me that we spent all that time, effort and money on him, but on reflection, that is what makes us better than him and his type.

It was soon time for the show, and as there was no microphone or sound system, I just had to talk loudly. I was quite surprised to see about forty people in the audience, but some of them were Russian, some were German and some were French. Most understood English, but it is hard to entertain them when they take time to translate it in their heads. But the British lads really made me feel welcome. I opened up with the line, "I'm not the comic, I've just come to see if Rudolf

Hess wants to buy a burglar alarm system." Which got a laugh, but Mr. Tactful, Brian, was stood at the side of the makeshift stage sweating and chain-smoking. He kept shouting at me to be careful what I said, as he was frightened that I might go too far, and he would have to pay a lawyer to get us out of there. Typical agent!

Everything went fine, and no lawyers were needed. We did the six shows in various barracks in the area and returned home a little bit less naïve, and a bit more educated in Nazi war criminals.

With Brian at the helm, I began working clubs that were more suited to my act. I still wasn't the outrageous comedian that I became, but I was getting there. I would still have to work a clean act one night, then my blue act the next. Some people were easily offended in those days, can you imagine what they would think today.

Of course you can't please all the people all of the time, and like every act working anywhere, you get good and bad nights.

# *Steve Pinnell*

I have known Steve Pinnell for many years. He's a great drummer and he plays all over the world with the band, "Smokie." I love him to death for a couple of reasons, firstly he laughs at my jokes, secondly because he is a great mate. I was playing golf with him one day, and I'm not a very good golfer. I teed off, and hit the ball straight into the woods. So I put another ball down and promptly hit that straight into the water. I tried again, but this time I missed the ball completely, so I turned round and in fun, threw my club at the golf cart and kicked my golf bag whilst shouting, "Fuck it" at the top of my voice. Steve turned to me and said, "Why do you play golf Roy?" I said, "Well it relaxes me." That was it; Steve was on the floor holding his sides laughing.

Steve's wife, Val, was the sister of Brian, my first manager, and when I first went solo, Steve used to drive me around. Whilst coming back from a gig one night, we were travelling along the A19 when a police car pulled us up. Steve was shitting himself, as he had never been in any trouble in his whole life, he wouldn't say boo to a goose. The officer came to the window and said to Steve, "I hope you're keeping one eye on the road and one on the Speedo." I'd had a drink, so I said, "You'd better make up your mind as to which is more important officer, because he's only got one eye, AND he's had a drink." Steve went white; he was shaking so much that if I'd put my washing inside his trousers, it would have dried in 10 seconds flat. I was on a roll, so I said, "If you're going to book us, could you hurry up officer, because my friend here is on some very strong drugs." The policeman looked shocked and asked what he was taking. I said, "Laxatives, so if you don't hurry up, he's going to shit himself." The copper laughed and sent us on our way. I don't recommend anyone using that line on a policeman, because they don't always see the funny side, and you might get yourself locked up for the night.

# *Onstage Stories & Ad-libs*

I assume that if you're reading this book, then you know that I have always been a little bit suggestive on stage. Comedians today keep using the phrase, "Breaking the boundaries." Well I've broken them all my life. When I started doing the working men's clubs, bad language on stage was taboo. I would have to adjust my material as I went on because I knew that some clubs would let you get away with a bit more than others. However, I could still get it badly wrong, like the time I told a story about picking up a prostitute. The gag was that she let me use a vibrator up her arse whilst I was shagging her, and it turned out to be the most expensive experience with a prostitute that I'd ever had, because she made me pay for the batteries and they conked out ten times during that session! Needless to say, I left the club by the toilet window that night. How I ever got paid, I'll never know.

In those days, a gig was a gig, and that's how I made my money, so I would take anything on just to put food on the table. Brian, who was my manager at the time, rang me up with a gig. He explained that it was at Peterlee Catholic Club, and was a Men Only event. He told me who to speak to when I got there, and who would pay me. I was happy, because I was going to get paid on the night and not have to wait for it. I arrived and was shown to the Gents' toilet where I was to get changed, and yes, there was piss all over the floor! I was on at 9.00pm and after about ten minutes a voice that was louder than an elephant's fart, shouted out, "I seen you at Hartlepool last week Chubby, how about telling us something new." The room fell silent, as I looked at the bloke and said, "Why don't you fuck off, fart-face." He answered straight back and said, "That's new!" the audience roared with laughter, and I got into my stride. That's a great example of when a heckle works fine. It's when somebody just shouts drunken abuse at you that it doesn't work, and the rest of the audience gets bored of them, and if they won't shut up, it can ruin the night for everyone.

Heckling is a strange thing, and a good heckle can lead to some good ad-libs, but some people think that they can beat the comedian with a line we've all heard, and dealt with, hundreds of times. The usual one is when someone gets up and shouts "I'm off to see if the comic has turned up." Let me tell you, I, along with every other comedian in the country, have 1001 answers to that line. I used to say, "Wait for me then, I'll come with you." Or, "good, cos I'm not the comedian, I'm a brain surgeon but I couldn't do fuck all for you, you fucking empty-headed bastard!" Or, "If he's arrived, could you get him to come into the concert room and see if he can make these miserable bastards smile." So remember, if you're going to heckle, be original. Johnny Hammond told me about a time he was working in a club in Liverpool, where a woman kept shouting out. He said, "Do us a favour lads, will someone go over there and stick a cock in her mouth to shut her up." Quick as a flash, the woman in question shouted, "Yooo Hooo, I'm over here." Now that's funny.

There are times when a comedian gets the chance to heckle, mostly at other comedians' funerals. When Timmy Taylor died, many of the club comedians were at Acklam Crematorium for his funeral. Timmy was a popular comedian on the circuit, and the place was packed. The service was quite moving, and we were all upset at his passing. As the coffin slowly moved behind the curtains, it got stuck. Johnny Hammond, who was stood next to me, said, "Bloody typical, you could never get him off stage when he was alive!" We all laughed, and I'm sure he would have done too, wherever he was.

Can you imagine what it was like at Bernard Manning's funeral? The place was full of comedians; it was like a who's who of the comedy world. Cannon & Ball, Frank Carson, Stan Boardman, Jim Bowen and the list goes on. I went with Steve Cowper, but was on a very tight schedule, as I had to get to Oxford for my show that night. Bernard arrived to a round of applause in a horse-drawn hearse. His coffin had his car registration plate, 1 LAF attached to it. It was one of the most moving funerals that I have been to. During the service, Bobby Ball and other people close to Bernard did readings. Frank Carson kept heckling, and then he stood up to address the congregation. "They say Bernard was a racist," he said. "Well how can he be, he's just had four black horses bring him here!" The place was in uproar, and everyone wanted to chip in. What a fitting way for him to be "sent off." I do miss Bernard.

# The Unforgettable Fight Night

Every entertainer has shows that they'd like to, but never can, forget. I have lots of those, but this one does stand out. I was on stage at the Richardson and Westgarth Social Club on the roundabout at Hartlepool when a fight broke out. To be honest, I was involved and this is what happened. I was in the middle of my act, when a heckler shouted out, "Why don't you fuck off home, you Geordie bastard." I immediately said, "Why don't you pawn your shirt and buy a fucking map. I'm not a Geordie, I'm a Yorkshire man." He then said, "Aye, and you're crap, you big fat cunt."

Well, in the heat of the moment, I decided that diplomacy was the best course of action in this situation, so I stepped down from the stage, walked over to him and diplomatically hit him over the head with the microphone. He looked stunned, but managed to stand up and throw a punch at me. So, again, I acted diplomatically and threw a bigger punch. It was at this point, diplomacy failed as his two brothers joined in; I didn't realize that they were sat next to him. All hell broke loose, and there now seemed to have been more punches than jokes that night. The police were called, and when they arrived the fighting had escalated, so they got stuck in and more punches were thrown. In fact, when I look back, it's a wonder that I have any teeth left!

Eventually, order was returned, and to be quite honest I was relieved that I hadn't been arrested. In my mind, it was a small victory for me and was feeling quite good. But as I walked out into the car park, my heart sank. My little van was sat there, but instead of being parked on its nearly new tyres, it was resting on four piles of bricks. Those brothers had got the last laugh.

# "IF" in "F"

I got a phone call from Johnny Hammond asking if I'd like to meet up for a drink at a gig he was doing in Middlesbrough town centre. It was at an old Jewish Synagogue that had been converted into a club called "Masters," and, of course, I said yes. When I got there, there was an old, tatty piano on the stage, and Johnny said to me, "Do you know the song, "If", by a band called Bread?" I said yes, and he asked if I would accompany him on stage by playing "If" in (the key of) "F." I said that would be fine by me.

Johnny wasn't on until eleven o'clock, so we stood at the bar and had a couple of drinks whilst watching the punters. The club had a reputation as a bit of a knocking shop, and was always full of old tarts trying to get a shag and old guys looking for the same. You could spend hours just watching it all going on. But all too soon, it was time for Johnny to go on stage. I was sat at the piano as he called for me to play, "If" in "F," but the joke was that he started singing it in B flat, and tried to find the right pitch as he went on. It was very funny, but one of the punters just didn't get the joke. He stormed up on to the stage and said to me, "Get off that piano you fat cunt, you're shite!" He thought I was ruining Johnny's act and wasn't happy with me. Johnny tried to rescue the situation by playfully slapping the bloke on the side of his head, but this enraged him even more. He turned around, and hit Johnny, so I hit him. Then he hit me and in the confusion, Johnny hit me and I hit Johnny. Then, the bouncers joined in and someone hit one of them over the head with an ashtray. Here I was in a fight again that wasn't my fault. In the middle of all this, I heard Johnny shout, "Chubby, get back on the stage and start playing the piano again or I might not get paid!"

I really miss Johnny Hammond; he was such a funny man who should have been a big star. Unfortunately, he was one of those blokes who just wouldn't do as he was told. When he was getting a bit of interest from the TV people, he should have played things their way, but he wouldn't listen to them. He had his chance, but it just wasn't to be for him. He did, however, turn his hand to writing, and used to write gags for comedians and for TV shows. It was a very sad day when he passed away.

# Billy Kelly – The Stripper & The Snake

Billy Kelly was another comedian from the North East, and we were good friends. He was one of those good-looking bastards, and he was never short of a fuck. We would often frequent the bar at The Fiesta Club in Stockton, where we would chat about the business and catch up on what was happening in our lives. He was a very funny man, and his version of the night he had spent with a stripper had me in stitches. It started when I asked him if he'd been working that week, and he told me that he had done a stag night in Newcastle the previous Wednesday.

Apparently, he had been on with a stripper called Lola who I knew quite well as we had worked together several times. She was quite large "up top," and I really fancied her, but had never managed to get a fuck. Well, Billy, being the handsome bastard that he was got lucky on this night. They went back to her flat in Gateshead and proceeded to indulge in some serious foreplay. Then, as they lay on the bed shagging, he felt something touch his foot, but he ignored it and carried on with the job in hand. He again felt something touch his foot, so he flicked his leg and cleared it away, but it wasn't long before he felt it again. This time, it was more like a tickle. He looked down and got the shock of his life when he saw a large snake sticking its tongue in an out whilst exploring his foot. It turned out to be Lola's co-star, a 5ft boa constrictor that had escaped from its basket.

THE SNAKE & Billy

Now, I know one thing for sure, I would have been out of that flat like a shot, but when I asked Billy what happened next, he told me that Lola explained that it wasn't dangerous and that it certainly wouldn't be attracted by the smell of the shit coming from his arse, and that it was unlikely to attack his goolies! So, he carried on shagging. I couldn't believe it as I asked him how he managed to carry on with a snake in the room. He told me that it was easy because he was in the middle of the vinegar strokes and was too excited to stop. I said "Didn't the snake put you off?" He replied, "No, it just made me cum quicker!" I laughed my bollocks off.

# The Stag Night

I was watching TV the other night and was quite shocked to hear Jimmy Carr using the word "Cunt." It's funny how times change, because I was considered too rude for TV and effectively banned from appearing on anything. Now, if you don't say, "Fuck" on a comedy programme, you might get dropped from the show! You have to bear in mind that what I was saying on stage was considered very offensive in the 1970's. I was controversial before Frankie Boyle had even started at school. In fact, one newspaper blamed me for "Bringing the building site on to the theatre stage." I suppose that was meant to be insulting, but I was proud of the fact that I entertained builders, factory workers and the majority of the working class.

I was described as a "Man's entertainer" and that's exactly what I was. I was used to working at "men only" functions, and I was good at it. My act developed through working on "Stag Nights" with strippers who did "Extras" for extra cash collected on the night. I mean; I couldn't go on after they'd been playing with dildos and licking each other out, and say "Have you heard the one about Pat & Mick going into a pub?" I would have been slaughtered.

Talking about this reminds me of the time I was booked to appear at The Police Officer's Christmas Party at a club in Seaton Carew, and when I say Police Officers, I actually mean Police *Men*, as it was a Stag Do. When I arrived, the club owner pulled me to one side and said, "Chubby, have you heard the phrase whatever happens in Vegas stays in Vegas?" and he gave me a knowing wink. I said, "Oh yes, but we're not in Vegas, we're in Hartlepool," and gave him a knowing wink back. You never know when you might need a favour from a policeman.

Soon, three girls arrived. They were from Nottingham and had a minder with them who looked just like Rod Stewart. I introduced myself, and we all went to the dressing room, which was a small area at the back of the stage that had a tatty curtain around it. We all had to share this area, and I for one wasn't complaining. I was only on £75, and for that I also had to act as compere for the night. The girls however, were each getting £200. They were all really nice, and as we were chatting and having a laugh, I turned around just in time to see the best looking one of them rubbing cream all over a rubber cock, an image that became imprinted in my memory.

The show started at 10 o'clock, and by 12.30, I might as well have been talking to the crowd at an FA Cup Final, it was that noisy. They were shouting and encouraging their mates to get up with the girls, it was a free-for-all on that stage. It was the nearest thing to a Roman Orgy that I'd ever seen, as many of the policemen had their truncheons out! The girls were simulating sex, and groping the guys' dicks. I turned to the bloke next to me at the bar and said, "Well at least we won't get raided by the Police." He said, "I should hope not Chubbs, cos you see that bloke over there in the white shirt, waving his cock in the air? Well that's our Superintendent!" So much for the long *ARM* of the Law.

# A Night of Hairy Pie

One of my early cassette tapes was called "Hairy Pie" which, for those of you who don't know, is a term of endearment for the Lady Garden, or Minge/Mott/Split/Gash/Fanny, you get the picture. Anyway, I had been booked at Thornaby Social Club, which was at an old airfield. It was always a good night, so I decided to record the show.

When I turned up at the club, I found out that this was a "Hen Night" and that I was on with some male strippers. There was an audience of 600 screaming women, and as I was introduced, the noise was frightening. They started chanting, "Get your cock out for the girls!" and, as I approached the microphone, one woman shouted, "Show us your cock you fat fucker'." I have to admit, I was quite shocked. I mean wanting to see my cock was one thing, but calling me fat was totally out of order! But I wasn't about to give up on this show, because I'd already laid out money to record it. So, I opened up with my usual, "Good evening girls, my wife's got two cunts, and I'm one of them!" They loved it, and were cheering, jumping up and down and flashing their tits and knickers at me. I did a 45 minute show that night, and had a "hard on" for every one of those 45 minutes.

Midway through my act, a bloke walked into the room. He was obviously looking for his wife. Unfortunately for him, she was sat right at the front with her mates. He spotted her and marched straight over. I'm guessing that she had told him she was going to the bingo with the girls, and he wasn't too pleased when he realised that she was here. He grabbed hold of her and said, "Hey, you fucking cow, come with me!" and started to drag her out of the room. Without warning, the other women turned on him. It was just like a scene from one of those nature programmes, where a pack of hyenas take down a defenceless zebra. He didn't stand a chance. They were punching, kicking and scratching him, whilst the others were cheering them on. In an effort to keep the peace, I said, "Hey! There's no fucking dancing when I'm on," but it didn't seem to do any good. He eventually had to retreat from the room to lick his wounds.

I carried on with my act, but as I was the only man in the room, I became the target for anti-male venom. The heckling started, and a woman stood up and shouted something at me. I couldn't help noticing that her chest was flatter than cheap lemonade, so I said, "Did you know that the Red Indians used to attack women and cut their tits off to use as tobacco pouches?" Then I pointed straight at the heckler and said, "You'll be OK pet; they wouldn't bother attacking you, you fucking beanpole!" She laughed, and so did everyone else. I had managed to get the attention back on me, and the rest of the act went really well.

A few days later, I listened to the recording, and it sounded great, so I made the decision to release it for sale at my shows. But what should I call it? There was only one title in my mind, Hairy Pie! I thought it was a fitting title for a show performed to an audience of "Split Arses."

# *The Nightingale*

Before Pete started working for me full-time, I asked him if he would drive me to and from a gig in Birmingham. He was happy to do it and it meant that I could have a drink at the club. I hadn't worked at The Nightingale Club before, and I didn't know what to expect.

We arrived at the club quite early and as we approached the main entrance, the "man mountain" of a doorman greeted us. He did look quite intimidating; he was black and must have been about 6ft 6ins tall and about the same wide! He looked us both up and down and asked who we were. I explained that I was the comedian for the night, and Pete was my driver. His attitude softened and he told us that I wouldn't be on stage until quite late. I asked him where the dressing room was, but he said that there wasn't a dressing room; I would have to get changed in the ladies' toilets. He also explained that there was a "Pool Room" where we could have a drink and relax until I was due on stage. As we entered the club, it was quite noticeable that this wasn't the type of club that I normally worked. It was full of men with "Freddie Mercury-style moustaches" wearing leather trousers; some of them were even wearing frocks! I looked back at the doorman and said, "They're all Puffs!" He said, "Well it takes one to know one...Fatty" and gave us a wink.

We made our way to the Pool Room where we had a few games to kill the time. Pete was a little concerned about the surroundings, and he never once bent over the table to take a shot! In fact, in the car on the way home, he told me how uncomfortable he had felt in that club. I don't think he'd ever been that close to a gay man before. He needn't have worried, because nobody was interested in him, They were there just to have a good time with their partners.

I must admit that as I didn't know that I would be working in a gay club, I wasn't prepared. I had never worked in this type of environment before, and didn't know how to handle it. For the first ten minutes of my act, I took things carefully, trying to find a way to entertain them, but it wasn't going well. Suddenly, from the back of the room, I was heckled. The campest voice you can imagine shouted, "Fuck off back to the North East you fat bastard." Quick as a flash, and without thinking, I replied, "If you don't shut up, I'll have you put back where you came from and have the bloke's arse welded up!" The room fell silent, but after a split-second it erupted with laughter and cheering. I then realised that this audience were just like any other. They loved having the piss taken out of them, and I was certainly the man for that job. I now knew how to work this crowd, and when I finished, I got a standing ovation. I really enjoyed myself on stage that night.

After I left the stage, I got changed and had a quick drink at the bar, and everyone was saying how much that they had enjoyed the show. Pete, however, was itching to leave, he just felt uncomfortable. As we were leaving, the club owner came up to say thank you and asked if I was available the following night. I apologised and told him that I was already booked, so couldn't do it for him. Pete was stood next to me, and I smiled to myself as he just kept saying, "Yes he's working, he can't do it. Definitely can't come, he's working." Pete is a big strong bloke, but he was scared of these camp men, it was so funny to see.

Eventually, Pete started to work for me full-time. I was working the theatres, and needed somebody to take over from Ronnie when he left. We travelled all over the UK and the time came for the Summer Season in Blackpool. Pete now came into contact with Blackpool's "Showbiz people." As you can imagine, some of them can be quite camp. To my surprise, Pete just accepted them for who they were. You have to remember that he came from a small town, and had worked with blokes who were "men's men," so to speak. So, when he found himself in that gay club in Birmingham, he was totally out of his comfort zone. To his credit, he learned to accept people for who they are, and not for what he might have thought they were.

# *A Jollees Night*

In January 1982, I was booked to a "Men Only" night at a club called "Jollees" in Stoke-on-Trent. This was something that I was used to doing, and I was very good at them. But this was no ordinary night; I was the support comedian to the one and only Bernard Manning. He was the master of these types of nights, and I was a bit nervous about meeting him. Pete Richardson drove me there that night, and helped me sort everything out for my act.

Bernard arrived, and to me, it was like meeting God. This man was a legend, and here I was on the same bill as him.

He was so nice to me, and from that day, we got on great. We swapped phone numbers and became close friends. But it wasn't until many years later that he told me that he had vowed never to have to follow me on to stage, because he didn't think he would be able to do it. He also admitted that on that night in Stoke, he had pinched one of my cassettes so he could nick some gags. That was probably one of the highest accolades any blue comedian could get.

# Don't Swear at The Troops

Nowadays, we all have the utmost respect for our armed forces. They do a wonderful job and are a credit to our country. But when I was still doing the club circuit, we would often get sent to do gigs at Army bases, and I can tell you that none of the comedians respected them then. Junior ranks clubs were the worst. We would go on stage to a barrage of abuse. The lads were there for one thing, and that was to get as drunk as possible in as short a time as possible. You can imagine what those nights were like.

Well, I was given a gig to do at Catterick Garrison and had to be there by 8.00pm. I wouldn't be picking up any cash on the night for this gig; the agent would pay me later. I was given a letter with the details of the gig on, and it said, "Please be there by 8.00pm, refreshments will be provided. The comedian will not use any profanity, make no reference to the regiment and don't mention The Falkland's Conflict."

I duly arrived, and was taken to the Officers Mess, but as I wasn't wearing a tie, I was shown to a small room at the back where I would have to wait until I was due on stage. The room could have doubled as the broom cupboard as it was so small, but at least it had a window. My refreshments arrived and I was able to watch all the Top Brass arriving in chauffer-driven cars. They were all dressed in red tunics and their wives were in ball gowns and soldiers were there to open the car doors for them. It certainly looked like a posh do, and I was working out which of my clean material was going to work for such an event.

Eventually, there was a knock on the door and a sergeant came into the room. "We're ready for you Chubby," he said, so I followed him. We went out of the room, down a corridor, out of a side door, along an alleyway and into a different building. He asked me to wait there and he would get me introduced, then I could walk in and straight on to the stage. As usual, I checked my flies and psyched myself up for being super clean. I listened carefully at the door as I was introduced as Britain's bluest, dirtiest, filthiest comedian, Roy "Chubby" Brown. There was a massive cheer as the door opened and I walked in to 250 drunken squaddies. The abuse that was hurled in my direction was shocking. Chants of "You fat cunt" and "Fat fucker" rang around the room. It was quite shocking, I had never been subjected to that amount of abuse before. My face must have been a picture. I had to respond with everything I had in my armoury; it was the only way to get through to them. They were like a bunch of animals that night, and I must admit that I ignored that letter telling me what I could and couldn't say.

These sorts of gigs are hard to deal with, but by this time, I had gained a reputation, and I had to live up to it. There would be many more nights like this one, and they definitely made me work harder. Apparently, at that time, I was one of the few comedians who could handle these types of gigs. I'm also guessing that I was one of the few who would actually agree to do them, even though I thought it was going to be a posh evening for officers!

# The Maltese Motorbike Incident

I have been friends with Peter Richardson for over thirty years now, and he has worked for me, on and off, throughout those years. In fact, his wife, Lynne, makes all of my patchwork suits.

Needless to say, we are still close friends to this day. Everyone who knows him will tell you he is a gentle giant, and I wouldn't disagree. I have lots of great stories about Pete, but this one is my favourite.

Pete and Lynne, Beryl and me all went on holiday to the island of Malta.

Beryl
Nice Tits

The weather was fantastic, and as the island is so small we decided to hire some motorbikes to travel around and see the sights. Now, if you have ever been to Malta, you will know what we didn't know at the time; the roads are very dangerous! Not only are the local drivers totally mad, but also the roads are full of potholes. Anyway, like lambs to the slaughter, we went to the Motorbike Hire Shop, paid for the bikes, and had to leave a further £25 "deposit" in case of any damage.

As we set off, the sun was shining and we knew we had made the right decision by hiring the bikes. We headed to the famous "Blue Grotto" and when we got there, it was idyllic. The sea was deep blue and there wasn't a cloud in the sky. We went in a boat that took us in to the actual Blue Grotto, and then had something to eat from a mobile chip shop that was parked up in the small car park. It was now time to head back, so Beryl and I set off first, closely followed by Pete and Lynne. By now, I was getting confident on the bike, so I opened the throttle and whizzed of around the bend in the road. Pete, with Lynne on the back, was a bit more careful as he followed. As he rounded the bend, I was nowhere to be seen. Pete said afterwards that he was confused as Beryl and I just seemed to have vanished. He stopped his bike, and could here us moaning in pain. We had driven straight in to a massive hole in the road. There hadn't been any warning signs, bollards or anything. Pete stopped to help us out, and we were both injured. I was bleeding and Beryl was in a lot of pain. Luckily, a car stopped and offered to take us to the hospital in Valletta, an offer that we took up. Pete told us not to worry; he would sort the bikes out. Of course, mine was in a bit of a state, with a buckled wheel, bent handlebars etc. but that was the least of my worries.

When we got to the hospital, to my surprise, we were given raffle tickets. When our numbers were called, we could see a doctor. Eventually, I was called in, and the doctor was sat behind his desk, but bizarrely, just a few feet away was a workman stood on a table, cutting a pipe on the ceiling with a hacksaw. There was dust and shit everywhere. It certainly wasn't like a British hospital, but we needed treatment, and this was our only option. After a short examination, the doctor then took me to another room. I had a cracked rib, a broken toe and my arm was also broken. He put my arm in plaster, gave me some painkillers and sent me on my way.

Back at the hotel, my arm was hurting more and more, and I couldn't feel my fingers. In fact, they were turning blue. Beryl was so dosed up on painkillers that she wasn't much use. She had sprained her wrist and broken her arm too. So I got some nail scissors and started cutting away at the plaster. It took nearly two hours to remove, but when I finally got it off, the relief can only be likened to finally having a shit when you have had to hold it in far too long! The colour slowly came back to my fingers and the pain eased.

The next morning, we had to take the bikes back to the hire shop. I knew that I would lose my deposit, but at least I was still alive. As we went outside, Pete had a self-satisfied grin on his face. I was amazed to see my bike had all been straightened out. Pete had worked miracles, he had spent the night using his brute force and limited resources to get the bike looking as good as he could so I wouldn't lose my deposit. Now, he might be good with his hands, but he definitely can't keep a straight face, so we decided to go in to the hire shop separately, as I was afraid he'd look guilty and the bloke would notice that it had been in an accident. I needn't have worried, as they didn't even look at the bike and returned my £25 deposit in full. Pete looked like the cat that had got the cream; he was over the moon that we had got away with it.

It was now Pete's turn, so he kick started his bike ready to ride around the corner to the shop, but in doing so the kick-start pedal simply fell off, and it wouldn't go back on. The bloke in the shop noticed, and decided to go over the bike with a fine toothcomb, and he spotted a small scratch on the petrol tank. Pete came out of the shop with a face like an angry bulldog chewing a wasp. I asked what had happened, and he said, "That bastard's taken £10 out of my deposit to cover the damage." He was fuming, but all I could do was laugh. My bike had almost been written off, and he lost £10 for a scratch he hadn't done. Pete was fuming mad, and every time I looked at him, I laughed more. In fact, even now as I write this, I can see his angry face in my mind and I'm laughing. If you knew Pete, you would know that to him, losing £10 was like losing a barrel of free beer. He's never forgotten this incident and he's still angry about it. In fact, he's never been back to Malta because of it.

# Talent Shows

When I did the TV talent show, "Opportunity Knocks," Les Dawson and comedy duo, Little & Large were there. It goes without saying; I was a clean comedian in those days. Later, I went on to do the other big talent show, "New Faces," which produced loads of stars such as Jim Davidson, Marti Caine, Mick Miller and Cannon and Ball. This show had a panel of judges, much the same as "Britain's Got Talent" and "X Factor." I'm convinced that the only member of the panel who was actually alive on my heat was Tony Blackburn. For any entertainer, TV appearances are a big deal, and any criticism is like having a stake driven through your heart. I really wanted to be liked, and wanted my act to be perfect. Unfortunately, after a near-perfect performance, I finished off with a short comedy song at the piano, but halfway through, the piano lid fell down and trapped my fingers. I was devastated, I was convinced that I had ruined everything, but the audience laughed. They thought it was part of my act, so I smiled through the pain, and made the most of it. Then it was time for the panel to make their comments. My fingers really hurt, so I couldn't even cross them, I just stood there trying hard not to let the pain show. I don't really remember much of what was said, but I do remember Tony Blackburn saying, "I like this man, I just think he still needs time to develop, and I would like to see him do a longer set." I was happy with that. I wonder what he thinks of me now.

# The Drifters and the Platters

The Rendezvous Club in Liverpool was a place I played regularly. George, the owner, was a real character and a shrewd businessman. To give you an idea of how shrewd he was, I have to tell you the story of how he had booked "The Drifters." Now, in recent years, it seemed that any black man who could sing and dance and find four other black men who could sing and dance could call themselves "The Drifters." But back then, there was only one group of Drifters, and they featured the fantastic Johnny Moore. They had many hits including "Saturday Night at The Movies" and were a great live act.

George had booked them to appear at his Rendezvous Club, but ticket sales hadn't gone well. There didn't seem to be any reason for this, but sometimes it just happens. Unfortunately, he was tied into a contract that he couldn't get out of. If he cancelled the show due to poor ticket sales, he would have to pay their fee in full. So, being shrewd, he called up a mate who worked for the local electricity company. Then, on the day of the show, his mate and a couple of other guys turned up at the front of the club, erected a small yellow workman's tent and dug a hole in the pavement. The band was due at 1.00pm to set up their gear, so at 12.55pm he went to the fuse box and flicked the main switch to off. When the band arrived, he told them that there was a problem with the electricity supply and that he didn't know when it would be back working. Then, he took the band and their Tour Manager out to the workman's tent where he asked his mate what was happening and when the power would be back on. His mate pulled one of those workman's faces and said, "I don't think we'll have this working until tomorrow." George pretended to be angry and apologised to the band. "We won't be able to open the club tonight, so you might as well go home." The band understood that this was something out of his control, and their management didn't charge a cancellation fee. Now that's a shrewd club owner for you.

It was just a few days after this incident that I was working at the club, so I know it was true. In fact, they had only just filled the hole in. George was a lot happier by then because he had sold out for my show. All was going well, and I was having a great gig, until the fight broke out. It was like a cowboy film where they would have a good old scrap in the saloon. Chairs were being smashed and the legs were being used as weapons. It was really mad, but I can honestly say that the fight was nothing to do with me - for a change! I don't know what started it, but the police certainly finished it. Unfortunately, I got the bad press over it.

Whilst I'm on the subject of popular "black" groups, I have to tell the story of when I worked with "The Platters." They were another popular group who had their early hits in the 50's and 60's, but had changed their line up a few times since then. "Smoke Gets in Your Eyes" was their biggest hit, and it was now popular again because a reworded version was used on a TV advert for ESSO Blue paraffin. The opening line to the song was, "They asked me how I knew, my true love was true." Which was altered to "They asked me how I knew, it was ESSO Blue."

Some of the larger clubs in the North East used to book big name acts, and on this particular night, I had been booked as the support act to The Platters. They were very professional, and were very specific about how they were to be introduced on stage. They were going to stand behind the curtain as the music started, then, the compere had to say, "Ladies and Gentlemen," the music would then go into the intro for Smoke Gets in Your Eyes, and after the first long note, the compere was to say, "All the way from America," followed by the next bit of the music, then, "International recording stars, The Platters." During this introduction the curtain would slowly open and the band would be stood there in silhouette. The lights would then change, and their show would begin. It was simple, but effective.

You could feel the excitement in the room as Showtime approached. The Platters were in position, the band was ready and the compere stepped out in front of the curtains. At this point, I have to tell you that this was the night that Barry McGuigan was fighting for the

World Featherweight Boxing Title, and this is what happened. The compere, who sounded a bit like the actor, Tim Healy, with his strong Geordie accent said, "Laydeeees and Gentlemen," the music continued. "All the way from America," more music. "International recording stars." The curtains opened revealing the silhouettes of The Platters. Then, as it was all going so well, he said, "But before I bring on the turn, I just want to let you know that Barry McGuigan has won the World Title, the Darkie threw the towel in!"

You can imagine how annoyed The Platters were. Not only had this guy messed up their introduction, but he had also just insulted black people by referring to them as "Darkies." One of The Platters dropped his microphone on to the floor, marched forward and punched the compere square in the face. I can't say I blamed him, but the funny thing was that the compere didn't understand what the problem was. It was great for me to be working in a club and not being responsible for a fight.

Platters or Drifters all look the Same

# A Celebratory Night

One of the most memorable nights I have ever had in my career has to be the one at Marton Country Club. It was Sunday 4th January 1981 and was a special evening for the police. Several of the top brass from Scotland Yard were there to present bravery and other awards to the local officers. The atmosphere was great and the place was packed with about 600 policemen and their wives. There was a band playing dance music and I was due to entertain them at 9.00pm.

I was onstage and in full flow when somebody came into the room and discreetly spoke to one of the high-ranking officers. They both then left the room together. After a couple of minutes the officer returned to the room with two more policemen, and he walked right up to the stage. I thought that he was going to stop me and tell me I was crap and that they weren't going to pay me. But no, he calmly asked for the microphone, so I said, "You'll never get away with stealing my jokes, there's loads of coppers in here." People were laughing as he took the mic. But as he spoke, they fell silent. "Gentlemen, I have an announcement to make. At 7.15pm this evening a gentleman was charged with the murders of several women. I am pleased to inform you that Peter Sutcliffe is being held in custody in relation to The Yorkshire Ripper case. We have our man." The room erupted, they were shouting and cheering "We've got the bastard, we've got him." Then the champagne started flowing and I was included in their celebrations.

It turned into one of the best gigs that I have ever done. I did carry on with my act later, but don't remember much about it because I was so pissed. Nobody was bothered about my act anyway; it was all about catching The Ripper that night.

# Aberdeen Hotel

In the early days of touring theatres, I was in Aberdeen. Ronnie Keegan was driving for me. He was a great guy, but, like everyone, he did have his flaws. Some of his choices of overnight accommodation left a lot to be desired, but on this occasion, the venue had negotiated a very good rate with one of the nearby hotels on Union St. So, we arrived early and went to check in. I was at the reception desk giving my details, and, as the theatre had booked the room on our behalf, my room was under the name of Roy "Chubby" Brown. On hearing this, the three young women behind us stepped back about a yard or so. The "Chubby" Brown reputation had gone before me. I always have to explain to people that "Chubby" is an onstage character, and I am not that person in real life.

As we were there for a couple of days, I had a few things with me, so a porter helped me to my room. I should explain that it wasn't a very nice day. It was cold and foggy, so it was nice to get into a nice warm room. As we entered, it was quite dark, so the porter opened the curtains. I took one look out of the window and closed them straight away. My room looked out on to an old, eerie graveyard. Not only that, but the fog was swirling around the gravestones making it look like something out of a horror film. It was a Tomb with a view! I can tell you, I slept with the light on that night.

After settling in to my room, I went to the lounge and ordered tea and biscuits. The waitress was a bit apprehensive of me, but remained polite and courteous. My tea arrived; and I poured a cup out. At this point, a gentleman came over and introduced himself as the Hotel Manager. I invited him to join me, and he sat down. We chatted and I mentioned how some of the staff seemed a little uncomfortable around me, and told him that they needn't worry, because I'm not anything like my character. In fact, I have the utmost respect for the fairer sex. He then explained that a few weeks earlier, another well-known comedian had been stopping there. This man had walked in, gone straight to the reception desk and done the whole, "Don't you know who I am?" routine. He'd been obnoxious from the moment he had walked through the door until the moment he checked out. Which reminded me of a similar incident at a hotel in Wales. They had recently encountered another well-known "Blue" comedian who had walked straight up to the reception desk and said, "Which one of you slappers is going to give me a blow job tonight?" I won't name him, but he did have a well-publicised alcohol problem, so he may have been pissed at the time, but there's no need to act like that.

There's no wonder that some hotels are apprehensive of adult comedians staying with them. I felt I had to apologise for all of us, but the manager understood, and he must have put the staff's minds at rest, because we had no problems after that.

When we went to check out after our stay, I felt that I had made a good impression and was quite pleased with myself. That was until the manager called me to one side and said, "Would you ask your friend to put the clock back." I didn't know what he was talking about, so I turned around to see Ronnie in his big coat. I could see the outline of what looked like a huge dinner plate inside the coat. I just looked at him and said, "Ronnie, what have you got under there." Sheepishly, he opened his coat to reveal a big antique clock that had been hanging on the wall last night. I couldn't believe it and just said, "Ronnie, what are you doing, you'll get us jailed, you dozy bastard." Ronnie stood there with his best, "I'm only having a bit of fun," face on, and the manager laughed. He saw the funny side, and he got his clock back. I know that Ronnie nearly nicked a clock, but in the end he didn't, and we left with our reputation intact, unlike some other comedians.

# The Flaming Support Band

In the early days of doing theatres, we did have some odd support bands. We tried to find a band that we liked, and then keep them for a while. But occasionally we would have to use a different band. We were due to work in a theatre in Derby when the call came that our regular band had all caught a stomach bug and weren't able to work. George rang me with the news, and told me not to worry as he had managed to book a different band that had a very good reputation.

We were pleased with ticket sales and with 500 sold at £5 each, it meant that after expenses had been paid out, we were making quite good money that night. I was really happy as the band sound-checked, they sounded great. Showtime came, and the band went on stage and opened up with a song called "Fire" by "The Crazy World of Arthur Brown." They had asked for all the stage lights to be turned off so that the singer could do his fire-eating trick. He set some sticks on fire and blew some liquid out of his mouth, lighting it with the flaming sticks. It must have looked great from the back of the room, but the ceiling didn't look so great when it started to smoulder. The alarms went off and we had to evacuate the theatre.

After the fire brigade had given the all clear, we were allowed back into the theatre where we carried on with the show. I felt that I had to go the extra mile that night, and did extra time on stage to make up for the earlier events. The whole theatre smelled of smoke and burning wood. The audience really respected that we had carried on, when we could have just cancelled the show. They gave me a standing ovation, and I was over the moon.

A week later, I was sitting at home when the phone rang; it was George who had some bad news. The insurance wouldn't cover the damage to the theatre, so we would have to pay for it ourselves. Here I was doing theatres, I thought I'd moved on from working men's clubs where they didn't pay me because they thought I was crap. Now I was working for nothing to pay for the damage that I hadn't done. I guess I'm just unlucky.

# Early Years

Winsford Civic Theatre was a regular on the touring circuit for us. In the early days, Ronnie Keegan always used to find our accommodation for the night. As the show had got bigger, and we had a bit more money to play with, Ronnie was still driving for me and still finding the accommodation. Unfortunately, he still saw it as an expense that should be kept to a minimum. He would go out and look for the cheapest place to stay. Now, some B & B's can be really nice, but equally, some really cheap ones can be really bad. This particular night was one of the bad ones. We did the show, and headed off to the B & B to check in. We paid our £8.00 each, and went to the rooms. I'm not saying it was cold, but there was ice on the inside of the windows. "Don't worry," said Ronnie, "there's an electric fire on the wall, it'll soon warm up." So I switched the fire on, nothing happened! Upon further inspection, the fire was connected to a meter. 10p in the slot would make it work. All was fine until 15 minutes later, when the meter ran out and the fire went off.

After an hour and a half, I had no more 10p pieces, so I knocked on Ronnie's door. I was in search of 10p pieces, but Ronnie had run out as well. So we both knocked on Steve's door, he just looked blue from the cold. He had only had one 10p, and had been freezing for the last hour and a quarter. We hatched a plan; we could cut 10p piece sized shapes out of the Lino that was on the floor, surely these would work in the meter! But they didn't, we were all freezing cold, so Ronnie came up with a new plan. "What is it," I asked, but he just looked at me and said, "Watch." He went to the next room and shouldered the door open, stripped the bedding from the bed and brought it to me. He continued until we all had enough bedding to keep warm for the night.

Breakfast was at 8.00 am, we were all down early, so we could get a hot cup of tea inside us, and leave before they realised that we had broken into all the other rooms. But the funniest thing was that they had a mural of a Swiss mountain scene covering one wall. The other wall was festooned with Swiss bells and a set of antlers from an unsuspecting deer. We guessed that they might be more used to the cold than we were, but we didn't stop to find out.

# English or Geordie

I like Scotland, and in particular I do have a soft spot for Aberdeen. I've had some fantastic gigs up there at The Capital and latterly The Music Hall. In the early days we would stop in bed and breakfast accommodation, and had a few good nights being educated in the local whiskies. But as the shows began to make a bit more money, we would stop in nicer hotels, and I remember one night in a hotel on Union Street when George nearly got us all into big trouble.

After the show, we all returned to the hotel and gathered in the bar. A few drinks were taken and we were chatting and telling stories. We were maybe getting a bit loud, but we were harmless. A Scottish man was stood at the bar, and he seemed to be listening to our conversation. I really didn't take much notice of him, and I don't know what set him off, but he started making comments about us. George was getting more and more wound up by him, and I could see that it wasn't going to take much for him to explode. Eventually, the man made one comment too many about us being English. That was it, George shouted at him, "We're not English, we're Geordies." He then picked a bottle up and threatened the Scottish guy with it. Banger was stood nearby, and quick as a flash dragged George out of the bar and straight to his room. The Scottish man sloped away with his tail between his legs and our evening in the bar was over. I was quite shocked by the whole situation, and couldn't believe what had just happened.

(Beneath a Scottish Kilt is a real prick)

The next day, I was thinking about the previous night, and how it could have turned very nasty. But I started to smile to myself when I remembered what George had said, "We're not English, we're Geordies!" Well, he can speak for himself, because although many people think I'm a Geordie, I'm not, I was actually born in North Yorkshire. Banger is from Leamington Spa in the Midlands and Steve is from Scarborough. The only Geordie there was George. So if you are that man, I apologise for the Geordie. But I have to say as an ambassador for the Scottish nation, you failed miserably. It's a good job you're in a minority with your anti-English attitude.

# Les Dawson

I had the privilege of meeting the great Les Dawson on several occasions. The first time was in a hotel in St. Anne's near Blackpool, and was near where he lived. The hotel bar was like a pub, and was Les's local drinking haunt. He was a small, rotund man and was as dry as sticks. He was witty and very quick-thinking. We had a good chat that night, and he told me that he had followed my career ever since seeing me on "New Faces."

I was in awe of this man; he was such a clever comedian and was quite unlike anybody else that I had seen doing comedy. I couldn't believe that he knew who I was and certainly wasn't expecting him to say what he said to me. I respected Les and when he told me that he thought that I could have become one of the country's top TV comedians, if I didn't swear, I was amazed. He apparently loved what I did, and was very complimentary about my timing etc. I told him that I thought it was too late for me to change my style, as I had been building up a following and carving a niche for myself, but was grateful for his support and encouragement.

The next time I saw Les was at a club in Pontypridd. I was on around 9.00pm; Les was due on at 10.30pm. He remembered me, and it was as if we were long-lost friends. But the funny thing was that he was supposed to be on a low fat diet. His wife, Meg, had been trying to get him to live a healthier life, but Les loved a fry-up! When I went to his dressing room, he had a small Calor Gas burner, the type you would use when you were camping. On top of that, he had a frying pan and bacon and sausages ready to cook. He was just like me, and couldn't go without his home comforts; I mean we all love a bacon sandwich.

# Spain

The office had been approached to see if I would appear throughout the summer in a cabaret venue in Benidorm. I had already committed to Blackpool South Pier for the weekends, but they were happy for me to do midweek. In theory, it sounded like a good idea, so the deal was done, pending on a trial run over the Easter week. All was going well until we turned up at Manchester Airport. We had been booked on a Spanish airline and it was delayed. After two hours, our flight was called. We went to the gate and boarded the plane. All the usual announcements were made in Spanish first. We were about to move off from the gate, when the plane shut down. A Spanish announcement was made, and all the Spaniards started to unfasten their seatbelts. I didn't like the sound of this. Then came the English version. Something on the plane had just broken, and we were all to leave the plane. I'm not a great flyer at the best of times, so I decided that I wanted to get off the plane, get my suitcase back and go home. George talked me into waiting to see what was going to happen and they said that a part had to be flown in from Madrid, via Heathrow and then up to us at Manchester. We would be at least another five hours delayed, so I was now definitely all for giving up and going home. But George, being an agent, bought some whisky and a pack of playing cards. He wanted us to get over there, so he could still charge the venue a fee. If we were late due to a flight problem, that's not out fault, and we should be paid, he said.

Steve, Ronnie, George and myself sat in that airport for hours. Finally, we were called for the flight, and arrived in Alicante airport at some ridiculous time in the middle of the night. We managed to get a taxi to the venue and were greeted by a distraught owner.

He invited us in to what looked like a Wild West saloon after a fight. He explained that all the people with tickets had turned up and he had to tell them that our flight was delayed and there wouldn't be a show that night. Some of them had accused him of conning them out of their money, saying that I wasn't really booked and it was just a way of getting their cash. I felt really sorry for him and we agreed to stay over and do an extra night to make up for it. I will give him his due; he took it on the chin, cleaned the mess up and carried on as if nothing had happened. Needless to say, after that experience, we decided against doing the summer over there.

# *Jackie Charlton*

Former Radio 1 DJ, Mark Paige once asked me to play in a Celebrity Football Team against a team of old 'Boro Players, in aid of a local charity. I was, and still am a big fan of Middlesbrough F.C. so I couldn't say no. I was to be in goal and turned up for the match in my flying hat and goggles, football kit and wellington boots. All was going well until the other team forced a corner. The ball was kicked over to Jackie Charlton, yes, THE England 1966 World Cup winner *Jackie Charlton*, who made the perfect header. The ball was heading straight to the top left hand corner, so I just flung myself into the air in the general direction of that corner. My wellington boots went one way and my flying hat went the other, but somehow, I managed to get a hand to the ball and it went over the top of the post. The crowd roared, "Chubby, Chubby, Chubby" so I turned to them and took a bow.

Full of pride, I turned back to see Big Jack Charlton walking towards me. I could see that he didn't look too pleased. "You've just spoiled my moment of glory and I'll get you back for that you fat bastard!" he said. Well, I might be daft, but I'm not stupid, so at the earliest opportunity, I feigned injury and had to be taken off the pitch on a stretcher. Jack was fine with me after the match; it's just that people like him never lose that competitive streak which made them winners.

# Eric Morecambe

Many years ago, I was working at a venue in Dunstable and, as I had a few hours to spare I decided to do a bit of shopping. I wanted to find something special to fit into a space in my living room, so I asked someone where I would find a nice antique shop. They told me of a place in Harpenden, which was just a few miles away. So, after a short drive, I found myself at the shop. Sure enough, it was a fantastic shop and was in a really nice area. I had a good look around, but didn't find anything that I liked. As I left, I noticed that it was next door to a specialist Tobacconist shop. The window display contained collectable lighters and unusual smoking paraphernalia. I thought that I would have a look in to the shop, as I had a friend who collected interesting lighters.

As I looked around, I heard a voice saying, "Chubby, is that you?" I turned around, and it was the man behind the counter. It turned out that he was a fan, and had got tickets for my show that night. We got talking, and he said, "You're the second celebrity that we've had in the shop this morning, Eric was in earlier." "Eric?" I asked, and he informed me that Eric Morecambe lived nearby and had been in earlier to buy his favourite pipe tobacco. Now, it was my turn to be star-struck. Eric Morecambe was one of my all-time comedy heroes. "I wish I'd been here to meet him," I said, "What's he like?" The shop owner went on to tell me how nice he was, and that he always had time to chat to fans. I was so happy that he didn't have anything negative to say. He finished off by telling me where Eric's house was and convinced me that it would be OK to knock on his door.

When I left the shop, I was full of it, and plucked up the courage to call at the house. I was nervous as I approached, but I just thought that this would probably be the only chance that I would get to actually meet this legend of a man. I rang the bell, and a woman came to the door. It turned out to be his wife, Joan. I introduced myself and explained that I was only in the area for one day, and it would be a dream come true to meet the man himself. She was a lovely woman, and explained that I had just missed him as he was on his way to London for a meeting. I was disappointed, but at least I had tried. She then said, "Wait there a moment," and she went back into the house. When she returned, she had a signed photo of Eric, which she gave to me. I have cherished that photo ever since, and to this day it sits on my office desk.

Over the years, there have been many comedians, but to me, Eric Morecambe has to be one of the funniest, most inventive comedians of our generation.

# Glasgow

Glasgow has a reputation as a tough place for comedians to work. There are many stories about old acts working at the Glasgow Empire Theatre that have become legendary. One of my favourites is about the double act, "Mike and Bernie Winters." They would open their act with Mike coming on to the stage playing a clarinet. Then, after he had got so far into the tune, Bernie would pop his head out from behind the curtain and interrupt him. They had performed this act successfully all over the UK. However, the Glasgow crowd wasn't so easily impressed. As Bernie popped his head from behind the curtain, a lone voice shouted out from the audience, "Oh no, there's two of them!" It was all downhill from there.

The curse of Glasgow struck me in a different way. I was working at the Glasgow Pavilion Theatre, and had parked in the small road at the side of the theatre. I always had a good night at this theatre, and as usual, it was packed to the rafters. After the show I went back to my car to find that a window had been smashed, and everything of value had been stolen. I was particularly upset at the loss of a brand new hat that I had bought that day in a Glasgow hat shop. It was quite expensive, and I had bought it for myself as a special treat. Kay, who was the Compere on the shows, also had her car broken into and had lost some dresses and other valuables. Naturally, we called the Police, who turned up quite promptly. They took the details and then proceeded to tell me that it was my own fault for parking in the city centre after 6.00pm. This shocked me, because I had never had any problems in all my years of going there.

My first gigs in Glasgow had been many years before, when I was part of a show starring the brilliant Scottish comedian, Hector Nichol. He was Billy Connolly's inspiration, and it was easy to see why. Scottish audiences loved him, but he didn't really do much south of the border. I used to watch him every night, just to see a master at work. He was really nice to me, and would invite me to have a drink with him, and he certainly liked a drink. Unfortunately, at that time, I wasn't really a big drinker, but I did try to keep up with him. I spent the whole week in an alcoholic haze, speaking gibberish. As Hector had a strong Glaswegian accent, it was difficult enough for me to understand him when we were both sober, so what we talked about when we were drunk is anyone's guess.

I made some great friends in Glasgow during that time and we still keep in touch. They love to come to my shows, and for old-times sake, they love to throw bottles at me!!! But all joking aside, I love Glasgow and its people and that is why I was upset when those police officers told me it was my fault for parking in the city during the evening, because that isn't the Glasgow that I grew to love. I'm not saying that it is all sweetness and light, but on the whole, it's a great city with great people.

I think Glasgow Pavilion has to hold the record for the best complaint ever. Whilst I was on stage, a woman stormed out of the theatre and sought out the theatre manager. She wished to make a complaint about the show. She found him, and started to lay into him, at which point, my old manager and promoter, George Forster was passing along with Steve Cowper who at that point was dealing with merchandising and was the Tour Manager. The theatre manager said to the woman that if it was a complaint about the show, she should speak to the promoter who was now stood next to her. So, she turned to George and began shouting at him. Her complaint was that I had used bad language on stage, and continually used the words "Fuck" and "Cunt," and that it was disgusting. Before George could explain that there was a warning on the posters and on the tickets, she carried on by saying, "I wouldn't mind, but he was the same when we came to see him last year!" How thick can you get. She came to see me the previous year and didn't like the swearing. Then she bought tickets to see me again, and complained that I was swearing again! You can't win them all.

# Pete Richardson Selling the RUDE Tape

We were in Aberdeen at The Capitol Theatre on Union St. It was Pete's first trip that far north, and he isn't the most patient person on the planet.

The venue was massive, and was completely sold out. The doors opened at 6.45 and Pete was all set up and ready to sell the tapes and T

Shirts. Now, the Aberdeen people are all very nice and polite, but they do have an accent, and Pete couldn't quite get to grips with it.

BRAVEHEART

Drawing

It wasn't until we were in the hotel bar after the show that he told me what had happened. All was going fine, until one gentleman decided to enter into conversation over which tape to buy. Pete had tried his best, but confessed it was more of a guessing game as to what he was being asked. So, he just told him about which tape was the newest, which had certain gags on etc. The man thought for a while and asked for "The Rude one." Pete informed him that they were all RUDE, but the man again asked for the RUDE one. Pete was now getting a bit pissed off, and wanted to get the sale completed, so that he could serve the next person. So he reached into the box and gave him the newest tape. The man looked puzzled, and said, "No, not that one, I want the RUDE one!" Again, Pete pointed out that they were all RUDE, and that this was the newest one, but the man wasn't having any of it. Everyone was starting to get a bit pissed off, so the man behind him in the queue decided to step in.

It turned out that the first man was asking, in his strong accent, for the cassette with the RED cover. Yes RED, in strong Aberdonian, can sound like RUDE to us south of the border. So we have the 2nd man to thank for not letting this misunderstanding turn into an international incident.

# Bernard and the De Montfort Hall

For many years, I was banned from performing at Leicester's "De Montfort Hall," and this was due to my great friend, Bernard Manning. He had performed there and, being Bernard Manning, he did what he did. He had taken the mickey out of everyone, Scottish, Welsh, Americans and Blacks and Asians. To complete his repertoire, he had a go at disabled people, gays and lesbians and everyone else. Of course, Leicester, has a large Black and Asian community, who are very well represented on the local council. They took offence, and banned any "Adult" comedians (because they might offend someone.) This directly affected me, even though I hadn't done anything.

I don't want to get on my high horse, but if a local authority bans an act, or a play or a film from their area, that can't be right. It's censorship by just a few people against the majority. Do they think that adults aren't capable of making up their own minds? I mean, if I was going to perform in the local park, where anyone could see and hear me, I could understand. But when people have to make the effort to go and buy a ticket, and actually turn out on a cold, wet and windy evening to go to the venue, I think they know their own minds. They know what they are going to see, and wouldn't go if they were likely to be offended. We do, after all, live in a free country, with freedom of speech, though I sometimes wonder these days.

Anyway, after that little rant, I'll carry on. But before I do, I must tell you a little story about Bernard Manning. He was a tireless fundraiser for charities, and he raised millions of pounds throughout his life. Anyone who doubts this should have been at his funeral. I was there with Steve Cowper, and we were inside the church for the service. Hundreds more were outside, just to hear the service on loudspeakers. Representatives from all the charities that he had supported were there, and every one of them was singing his praises. Please don't believe the bad things that some sections of the press tried to label him. He was a kind, considerate man, who was always ready to help those less fortunate than him.

One day, I read in The Sun newspaper, that Bernard had gone on a sponsored diet in aid of a charity appeal. The story said that the paper would pay £1000 per pound that he lost. I knew that Bernard liked his food, so I thought it was a big thing for him to agree to do. Anyway, a few days later, I was travelling home from a gig down on the south coast, when we stopped at Watford Gap Services on the M1. As we pulled up, I noticed a huge Cadillac car in the car park with the registration number BM 1. It was Bernard's car, so I went in, just in time to see him paying for his massive plate of chips and about eight slices of bread and butter. I got a cup of tea and joined him at his table. He was pleased to see me, and we started to chat. I couldn't resist it, and said, "I thought you were on a sponsored diet." He just looked at me and said, "Fuck 'em, I'll just give them the money myself." I laughed, because although he would do a lot of things to raise money for charity, he just couldn't give up his food.

Back to the De Montfort Hall. After a few years had passed, and due to public pressure, my ban had been lifted. I was determined to give a great show. I wanted everything to run smoothly, so we hired local security and went ahead with the show. All was going fine, until about halfway through. Suddenly, this lad jumped up from his seat and made a charge down the aisle, screaming like a demented banshee. He then took a leap on to the stage, completely passing the security. I could see him now coming directly for me, and my old self-defense training came in. I was still holding the mic, so I just put my foot up, and as he got close to me, I kicked him. He went flying, and ended up in the third row, across the laps of three girls. At this point, their boyfriends took exception to him being there, so they started hitting him. Security moved in and dragged him out of the building. To this day, I have no idea what he thought he was doing, but I do know that Leicester City Council weren't too pleased. I was banned again!

# *Savva's*

I'm lucky to work in a business full of characters, and one of the biggest was George Savva. He had managed several of the major cabaret venues in the UK, including Caesar's Palace in Luton and Blazer's in Windsor. Eventually, he decided to buy his own club, which turned out to be just outside the small Welsh village of Usk. The nearest big town was Newport. In other words, it was in the middle of nowhere.

George, or Sav as we came to know him, had a fantastic reputation within the industry. He knew everyone. In fact, major names would work in this small club in the middle of nowhere, just because Sav asked them. Cliff Richard would do a week there, and tickets would just be sold to his fan club members. Apparently, they were amazing nights, and allowed Cliff and his band to prepare for big tours.

I had never worked for Sav before, but he was a shrewd businessman, and he had found out that I would sell a lot of tickets, so he booked me for three nights. All three nights had sold out, and I was looking forward to doing the venue. I travelled there on the day, and was proudly wearing my new set of denim overalls. The lads on the crew will tell you about my fashion sense. I thought I looked good, Pete and Steve were not so sure. Anyway, I arrived at the club, got out of the car after the long journey, had a good stretch, and headed towards the main entrance. As I was about to go in, a man was coming out, He took one look at me and said, "The bins are around the back, please don't come in the club in your overalls." I was taken aback, and didn't know what to say. For the first time in ages, I was lost for words. But, I pulled myself together and told him who I was. It was Sav, and he was so embarrassed at what he'd said. I never wore those overalls again, and have never let Sav forget our first meeting. Pete and Steve have never forgotten it either.

We all went into the club and had a cuppa, and from that moment on, we became firm friends. Sav was so impressed at the speed the tickets had sold and, as the club owner, he knew he was making money. He then told us that because our office had insisted that I would have to be on stage no later than 9.00pm, he had booked another act to perform after me. This was to keep the audience in, and hopefully keep the bar trade going. We asked him if he knew what to expect that night, and he said he knew what my act was like. But that's not what we meant; we were talking about the audience. He looked blank, so we told him that our audience did enjoy a drink, and that he should be prepared. He was convinced that everything would be fine.

The doors opened at 7.00 and the audience started arriving. I think every rugby club in South Wales had run a coach trip to see me. By 9.00pm they were like a baying mob. Roddy Miles, the compere at the club went on stage. Roddy was very well-spoken, and he had only just opened his mouth when he was shouted down with a barrage of abuse, questioning his sexuality. He did the quickest introduction of his career, and I was on stage. Quite honestly, it was a battle between the crowd and me but I did my act, and they loved it. I came off stage, and expected Sav to be there, but he was nowhere to be seen. He was busy helping out on the bars.

By now, the other act had arrived. It was Clive Webb, the mad magician. He was expecting to go on stage around midnight. His act is a bit "off the wall," and I did suggest to the powers that be, that this might not be such a good idea. But they wanted to run with it, so there was nothing more to say. I left and went to bed, as we were stopping in the accommodation on site. Steve, Pete and Banger decided to stay and see what happened.

Midnight came, and Clive Webb went on stage. I did mention that his act was "off the wall," and I'm not sure that the audience quite understood why he had a bloke with him on stage, whose only job was to hit himself over his head with a tin tray. He also had a very thin girl assistant. As he proceeded with his act, the audience were becoming more and more hostile. Beer mats were being thrown, and things were getting out of hand. But, ever the professional, or just plain mad, Clive carried on. He got to the point where he was going to cut the assistant in half with a big sword. The girl lay on the table ready to perform the illusion, and Clive said, "What shall I do with the sword?" The reply came back from one member of the audience, "Stick it up her cunt." at this point, Banger stepped on to the stage, grabbed hold of Clive and dragged him off. He had looked so wound up, and was holding a large sword, so Banger thought it best that he didn't get the chance to get at the audience!

The next day we had a meeting with Sav, who admitted that for the first time, he'd got it wrong. Not only had he made the mistake of trying to put another act on at midnight, but also he should have listened to us about the drinking. He had run out of beer, and had been to all the pubs in the area, borrowing barrels. But, he wasn't going to get caught out over the next two nights. He brought in extra bar staff, ordered emergency delivery from the brewery, and had employed someone just to be there to change barrels, as they were selling out so fast. He also decided not to use Clive Webb over the next two nights, and had paid him off. Sav was a happy man; his bar take had never been so high.

I mentioned that we were all stopping on site. Well that's another story. The accommodation was in the form of chalets. To be quite honest, they were a bit grotty, but you didn't have to drive to get there, so we could all have a drink. They were also very peaceful during the day; so all in all, it made sense to stop there. We continued to work at the club for many years, and one day I was in my chalet, with the door open. It was a beautiful sunny day, and a pigeon hopped into my room. It seemed so tame, so I fed it some crumbs. It went away, and came back with a friend. They seemed so at home, and I didn't mind them being there. I remember telling the lads about my visitors, but they that they hadn't had any in their chalets. The same thing happened each time I stopped in that chalet, but not in any other. Eventually, I mentioned it to Sav. He laughed and told me that that chalet had been converted from a pigeon loft, and that they must think they still have a right to live there! I wasn't so keen on getting that chalet next time that we were there.

# *This Morning*

When I started working in theatres, I became aware that my reputation was growing. On our first visit to a theatre we might only sell a couple of hundred tickets, but when we went back, we would be sold out. People were talking about me, and my tapes were being passed around which was spreading the word, and business was very good. Eventually, a deal was done with "Universal Home Video" and my first VHS tape; "From Inside The Helmet" was released. It was a huge success and, as a result, I was asked on to ITV's flagship daytime TV show, "This Morning" with Richard and Judy. I agreed to do it, and duly turned up at the studios at Liverpool's Albert Dock.

I know I've said it before, and I will say it again. I am not the same person as the character I portray on stage, and you would assume that people in TV would have the brains to realise that. Well, the producer greeted me, and I have to say he did look rather nervous. He reminded me that this was a live TV show and, as it was the morning, I wasn't allowed to swear or say anything that could cause offence to a daytime audience. I told him to relax; I wasn't stupid and wouldn't cause any problems. He thanked me and led me to the Green Room where the other guests for that day's show were sitting enjoying tea and biscuits. I sat down and looked around the room. There were a couple of actors who were there to promote a new TV series, along with some regular people who were there to tell an unusual story about themselves. But I was quite excited when I noticed some of the Coronation Street cast. "Corrie" was the biggest show on TV, and these people were massive stars.

The time came for my interview, and I was taken to the studio floor. I sat on a sofa and waited as Richard did the introduction. He said, "Next we have one of the most controversial comedians touring the UK today, and he has promised us he will behave himself this morning, Roy "Chubby" Brown." He then turned to me and started the interview by saying, "It's lovely to finally meet you after all this time, we've heard your tapes and watched your video." He was about to carry on, but Judy interrupted. "Well no, I haven't, I've never seen his video or listened to his tapes!" She was going bright red and she nearly choked on her words. I smiled and carried on with the interview, but as I looked at Judy, I could see her shaking. She was obviously worried about what I might say. But as I sat there, I could see straight over her shoulder, and what I saw was so funny. It was one of the Coronation Street cast who had obviously just been to the toilet before her interview. Unfortunately for her, she hadn't realised that her dress was tucked up into her knickers at the back. What made this funnier was the fact that Richard and Judy couldn't see it, and I was trying not to laugh out loud during a serious live interview.

When I got home, I watched a recording of the show with some of my family and friends. Everyone pointed out how uncomfortable Judy looked. I explained that it was because she was nervous about interviewing me, but of course, she had no need to worry, as I would never have done anything to embarrass them. As I continued to watch, I could see the point where I noticed the dress/knickers incident, followed by me trying not to laugh at this poor woman's embarrassment. I bet you want to know who the lady in question was; well I'm a gentleman and couldn't possibly tell you that it was Emily Bishop.

# Mr. Methane

Over the years, I have had many different support acts. They have mostly been bands, because that's what seems to work. But, I remember seeing a video of an unusual act and thinking, "mmmmm, he'd be good on the show." I spoke to George, and he booked him for one show in Swansea, to see if it would work. The day came, and we all were keen to welcome Mr. Methane to the show. He arrived in plenty of time, and set up on stage. He had a table, with a soft mat on it, and that was about it. If you haven't heard of him, and you don't know what he does, you should look him up on You Tube. He's a "Flatulist," or in plain English, he farts. Not just any old farting though, he can fart tunes and blow candles out with one gust!

Anyway, he introduced himself as Paul, and we had a chat. He's a lovely, very tall bloke from Macclesfield. He was very polite, and I remember asking him if he had much work. He told me that he worked two to three days a week as, in his words, "One's bottom can only stand so much." We had a chat, and he went to his dressing room.

The show was due to start at 7.30, and as it was getting close, I made my way to the side of the stage to watch his act. The audience didn't have a clue what to expect as he made his way on stage in a bright green, all in one, superhero-type suit with a large letter "M" where the Superman logo would be. He introduced himself to the audience, and proceeded to fart at will. He farted the National Anthem, then got everyone to sing Happy Birthday, before blowing the candles out on the cake. He put talc on his backside and farted, which then looked like the mushroom cloud after an atomic explosion. Amazingly, he even used a peashooter to fire a dart with a ribbon attached to it! The audience lapped it up, and I was in the wings, crying with laughter. It was the funniest thing I'd seen. I was still laughing at him when I went onstage.

MR METHANE ?

Roy Chubby Brown

I'm guessing that you might be wondering if we gave him the job as support act. The answer is no, he was just too fucking funny. It was just too hard to follow him. The whole crew couldn't believe what they had just seen.

I understand that he now works all over the world, and even turned up on the "Britain's Got Talent" auditions. Simon Cowell wasn't impressed; apparently he couldn't see him entertaining the Royal Family at the Variety Performance. Could you imagine if he did it and got nervous, he might just have shit himself!

# Dublin Gigs

I have regularly worked in Ireland, and the crew always enjoys Dublin. I'd like to think it was the culture, but in reality I think they like the Guinness. The first time we took the show over there, we were booked to appear at The National Stadium, which sounded very grand, but the reality was very different. It was a very old venue and was the home to Irish boxing; it was quite dilapidated and smelled of sweat. The dressing rooms were, to say the least, basic, and so was the auditorium seating. But we were there, and it was a sell-out, so the crew got the gear in and we were ready for the show.

I always like to do my shows early, because we sometimes have problems with people who use the evening as an excuse to drink too much. But this being Dublin, they have a very laid-back attitude to gig start times, and the local promoter had advertised the show as a 9.00pm start, which I wasn't too happy about. We eventually started the show at 9.40pm because the audience was only just trickling into the venue. Apparently, this was perfectly normal, as they don't want to see the support acts.

I was pacing up and down in my dressing room; I knew that this was going to be a tough gig. The late start meant that the audience had been in the pubs for quite a long time, and I had serious reservations about the venue. As my time came closer, I could hear the chanting of "You fat Bastard" and I was becoming even more concerned at how they would react when I finally took to the stage. As my intro music played, I felt like one of the boxers who normally fought in this venue. I walked on stage to a huge roar and immediately felt at home. When the lights went down, this was a fantastic venue to play, the atmosphere was electric and I loved it. The difference between the room in the cold light of day, and in the evening with a fired-up audience, was vast. I would certainly have no hesitation about playing there again.

The promoter, however, decided to change the venue, so we were booked to play at The Olympia Theatre in Dublin. It's an old theatre that has become famous for being the home of a national TV show as well as a great place for live bands to play. It's a building full of character, and that includes the stage manager. He had been there years and had seen it all. My crew loved working there, because everyone was so helpful and friendly. One time, when Shep and Ritchie were a little hung over from the previous night, the stage manager told them that he had some medicine to make them feel better. It turned out to be a cold can of Guinness! He also had a ready supply of the local Poteen, but I think that was a little bit too strong, even for our crew!

We would generally be at The Olympia for three nights, which gave us plenty of time to enjoy the city. I loved the shops, and would always buy some nice antiques for my home. These were the days before the Euro, and Pete was always on the lookout for a bargain. His eyes lit up when he found the local Irish Punt shops, "Puntland" and "Everything a Punt." I had to laugh.

One time when we were there, the theatre had one of its, "Midnight at The Olympia" gigs on. It was The Bootleg Beatles and, as I had heard good reports about them, I fancied seeing their show. Steve spoke to the promoter, and it was all sorted out. As my shows now started earlier, we were finished by 10.00pm, so the promoter said he would take us to his club in another part of Dublin and bring us back for the midnight show. We were driven to the club and taken straight to the VIP area where we ordered our free drinks. We were seated on a balcony and talking to each other as we settled down. There was a band playing, and they sounded very good, but we weren't taking much notice. Suddenly, they started playing the Paul Young hit "Wherever I Lay My Hat," and we all said how good the singer was. In fact he was just as good as Paul Young, so we took more of an interest. It was then that we realised that it was Paul Young! We didn't know that we were going to see a band, let alone one of my favourite singers of the previous few years. His band was one of the tightest I have ever seen, and his vocals were spot on. I thoroughly enjoyed their set, and as soon as they had finished, we were invited backstage to meet Paul and his band. I was like a kid again and was so nervous of meeting one of my musical heroes. I needn't have worried, Paul was with his wife, and we had a chat and a couple of photos together. It turned out that he did a lot of low-key gigs. He did them because he loved working with these fantastic musicians, and it wasn't about the money. I remember thinking that that must be a great place to be in your career, working for fun with talented people.

All too soon, it was time to get back to The Olympia for the midnight Bootleg Beatles show. I was looking at my watch, and thinking that we were leaving it a bit late, but the promoter assured me that we were on "Dublin Time" and a Midnight Show would probably start nearer to 1.00am. Sure enough, I seem to remember that it started about 12.45am. The band took to the stage in authentic Beatles' suits with "Mop Top" wigs. They had all the original instruments and amplifiers, so when they played, it was just like being back at that concert in The Middlesbrough Astoria in 1963. The difference was that the Bootleg Beatles played better than the Beatles had played on that night. I suppose when you think about it, they must have played these songs many more times than the Beatles actually played them. I have to say that I really enjoyed both bands that night; it was a pleasure to see two such good gigs in one night.

Dublin was also the only place that we had a police raid. It was bizarre, and came completely out of the blue. It happened just as the show had finished and Steve was in the main entrance selling the merchandise. All of a sudden, Garda Officers surrounded him. They informed him that they had received reports that we were selling illegal, obscene videotapes. Steve explained that the videos were all perfectly legal and that we purchased our stock directly from Universal Home Video. One of the officers then told Steve to show them all of the videotapes that we had with us. Steve had to oblige, and the officers then told him that they *were* illegal, and that they would be confiscating all of our stock. It turned out that although they were all legitimate and had the correct "Over 18" rating on the packaging, this didn't cover The Republic of Ireland. They explained that my videos hadn't been granted a certificate for sale there. They said that as a strong Catholic country, my material was too rude to sell on videotapes. I could perform live, but not sell the tapes! They must have confiscated over a hundred videos that night. I don't know what they did with them; I can only assume that they destroyed them. My DVD releases now have the correct certification for sale in Ireland.

# *Isle of Man*

The first time I worked over on the Isle of Man was an experience never to forget. It was where the comedy legend, Norman Wisdom, lived and has its own traditions, rules and regulations. The thing was, we didn't know that until we got there. The crew, my manager George and I flew over from Blackpool Airport in what could only be described as a flying coffin. It really did look like a coffin with wings on it! The support band took the ferry, as they had to bring all their gear.

We arrived at the airport and were met by the local promoter and a minibus. I wasn't expecting the warm welcome that I got from the airport staff. It took ages to get through because everyone was so friendly, and they treated me like some sort of superstar. We all got into the minibus for the short journey to the hotel, a journey that took us over "Fairy Bridge." But before we arrived at the bridge, the driver explained that there was a local tradition connected to it. Apparently, local folklore said that this was where the fairies lived, and everyone who crosses the bridge should say hello to them to ensure good luck. If you drove over without saying hello, you would encounter bad luck. We were, to say the least, a little sceptical, but the driver told us that unless we said "Hello Fairies" he wouldn't drive over the bridge. So, as we approached, he gave the countdown and most people on the bus mumbled "Hello Fairies." The driver, however, knew that someone hadn't done the greeting, and insisted that everyone should say it, or the bus would stop. Again, he counted down, but this time, we could here Banger using his best "I'm not gay, gruff, low-pitched" voice saying, "'Ello Fairies." Everyone looked at him and burst out laughing, and he just smiled. He didn't want to say hello to those fairies, but was under pressure to do it. The driver was now happy to proceed, and I'm still not sure that he wasn't having us on. I mean really, fairies under the bridge? Surely they have their own nightclubs to go to!

As we were over there for a couple of days, I decided to go shopping. I was still with Sandra at the time, and as I walked down the high street, I saw an outfit in the window of a shop that would really suit her. So, I went in, and asked the assistant for some help in buying it for her. She was showing me some choices of colour, and some options of accessories, when the door opened and in walked George. He'd been walking past the shop and seen me in there, so he came in. Before I could speak he said in his best camp-sounding voice, " OOOOOOO Cecil, that's lovely, I'm sorry I've spoilt your surprise." Then he looked at the assistant and said, "I hope he's got my size right, I'm down to a 14 now." I joined in the fun and carried the joke on, but the assistant looked uncomfortable with it. I bought the items, and we left the store hand in hand.

That evening, we were at the theatre and I was telling the story. The local promoter looked a bit uneasy. He then explained that in the Isle of Man (at that time) homosexuality was illegal, and was punishable by "The Birch." He also told us that if the assistant reported us, we could even be arrested at the airport when we tried to leave the island. I shit myself. Can you imagine the headlines in The Sun if that had happened. He later admitted that he was just winding us up, as the birch had been banned, but homosexuality was still illegal on the island. You can bet your bottom dollar that we said hello to the fairies for luck on the way back to the airport. Everything was fine, and we have been back there several times since, but have never tried the gay joke in shops again. And for the record, Banger really did say "Hello Fairies" every time we went over that bridge. Sorry Banger, but it's true!

# The Lock

The phrase, "Go to Hell" is often used, and has been said to me on many occasions. But let me tell you, I've been there; I've been married three times. Do you know the difference between a dog and a wife? The dog is always pleased to see you. I'm not bitter, but sometimes I'd rather have been in prison than married to my last ex-wife, because in prison, I would at least have been able to finish a sentence! I know these are bad gags, but I did have a bad time in this previous, well-publicised, marriage. It was one of those love-hate relationships where we loved to hate each other. I remember thinking about what my father said to me when I was a young lad. He said that you could never beat a woman, and he was right.

I had worked hard all my life, and managed to buy "Sunnycross House," the house of my dreams. I spent a fortune on buying it doing it up and making it perfect. Then this woman moved in, and we got married. We didn't have children, in fact looking back, at times we both behaved like children. We fought like cat and dog, and both had a thoroughly miserable time. I funded her lifestyle and she didn't contribute anything financially. She would check up on my every move. In fact when I arrived at the gym one day, the receptionist told me that she had to ring my wife to tell her what time I had arrived, and what time I had left. I could go on and on, but there is so much that I am not allowed to talk about.

When the marriage inevitably broke down and we went to court for the final settlement, she surprised me by showing that she could have been one of Britain's greatest actresses. In court, butter wouldn't have melted in her mouth and she completely convinced them that she should have the lion's share of my wealth. My father's advice was ringing in my ears as she got the house, the car, money and some of my treasured possessions. She even tried to get her hands on my prized "Steinway" piano, even though she couldn't play a note. I was devastated, but there was nothing I could do. My luck was definitely out that day; I must have spilled some salt whilst walking under a ladder, narrowly avoiding a black cat that crossed my path causing me to break a mirror! At least I'm not bitter!

When I look back at that marriage, I think of all the bad times, but behind those bad times, funny things happened. Unfortunately, my mates could get dragged into situations between her and me. One of these incidents involved my great friend Pete Richardson. He was working for me at the time, and would always be there if I needed him. I'm the sort of person who can't change a fuse in a plug, or change a light bulb. My head is full of jokes and there's no room left in there for practical stuff like that.

After a particularly bad row, my ex had stormed of out of the house. I knew that when she did this, she'd go to her mother's house, then her Auntie's. She would tell them all what a bastard I was, and then return home to make my life miserable for a couple of days. But this time, I'd had enough. I called Pete and asked him to come to the house and bring his tools and a bolt to fit on the back door. Reliable as ever, Pete arrived at the house with his tools and a shiny new bolt. I made us both a cuppa, and he proceeded to fit the bolt. He was just finishing, when the lady in question pulled into the drive. As usual, she had a face like thunder as she marched up to the back door. She had already told me that she didn't want Pete at the house unless he was picking me up to drive to a gig. This was because he was a close friend, and she had convinced herself that he was covering things up for me.

Whilst he was fixing the bolt on the back door, I had been and bolted the front door, so we were now both locked inside the house. She started banging at the newly-bolted back door, calling me all the names under the sun. In fact she used a few that were new to me so I wrote them down and used them in my act later on. Pete now realised why I had asked for the bolt. It wasn't for extra security, it was to keep her out. Although he will never admit it, he was as scared of her as I was. It's a good job that house was in the countryside and had no close neighbours, because our rows were louder than an AC/DC gig.

I was quite enjoying us shouting at each other through the back door, but Pete was thinking about how he could escape. After all, he would have become the target for her verbal abuse if she had got in. He managed to unlock the front door, and sneaked around to the side of the house to where his car was parked. He thought that he could get into it and escape, but he was wrong. She had parked her car directly behind his, so that he couldn't just drive off. I hadn't a clue as to what was happening to Pete by then, as I was involved in the biggest slanging match of my marital history.

It wasn't until a few days later that I found out that Pete had had to break into her car to release the handbrake and quietly push it out of the way. Bear in mind that she was only just around the corner shouting at me. He freely admits he was shitting himself, but managed to get into his car and drive away at speed. We laugh at this now, because it was the most ridiculous situation you could ever imagine, but it was just a normal day in my life. Of course, I eventually had to let her into the house, and as you can imagine, I was put through hell for the next few days because of what I had done.

# *Celebrity and Reality*

I once walked into the bar at The Village Hotel in Blackpool, and Katie Price, or "Jordan" as she was known at the time, was stood at the bar. I couldn't get over how small she was; she was like a midget. I had seen her in the papers and on the TV, and it's strange how we form an image in our minds of people that we see in the media. But when you see them in "real life," the reality is very different. I once met the Australian singer and actress, Natalie Imbruglia; she was the same, very small. Don't get me wrong, she was beautiful, but small, and I remember thinking that she'd be good for blowjobs, but not good for getting your ball off the roof!

When you get to meet your heroes, you never think that they have their own problems. I nearly cried when I saw Ken Dodd getting out of his car. I was told he suffered with arthritis and it was pretty obvious on that day. I felt so sorry for him, but as soon as his intro music started, he bounced on stage as if nothing was wrong. It's amazing what adrenalin does to the body, and there's no better way of getting an adrenalin rush than going on stage and making people laugh.

It was in The Village Hotel that I met Estelle. (I've just realised that rhymes!) She was a very nice girl who asked me for money, and when I refused, she went to the papers. Obviously there's a long story involved, so I'll tell you the basic version. She worked behind the bar, and was a very attractive girl. She had lovely eyes, and when she looked at me, we just sort of connected. I never in my wildest dreams thought that she would look at me twice, but she did. So, I asked her if she would like a drink, and that's how it all started. How it finished, was a completely different matter.

When she had finished work, she joined me for that drink. I was flattered, and felt really good. I used all my best lines on her. Some of them were really cheesy, but a standing cock has no conscience. We started seeing each other when I was in Blackpool. We went out for meals, and enjoyed each other's company. I was still married to Sandra at the time, but that didn't stop me seeing Estelle. She made me feel good, but what came next was a complete shock. She asked me for money, and I said no. I didn't think that was what this relationship was all about. Things immediately changed between us, and I got the shock of my life when I opened the Sunday paper and saw her photo. She was pictured in expensive lingerie, and I have to say she looked great, but it was the headline that got to me, "Chubby Brown kept his hat and white socks on whilst we made love." To make things worse, as I read this, Sandra was sat opposite me at the breakfast table. I closed the paper, took it with me, got into my car and fucked off as fast as I could. Sandra didn't even realise that I had gone until her auntie called her to tell her that it was in the paper.

Let's get things straight; I didn't keep my hat and socks on! She also said that I had seduced her several times and had made love all night long, which, like most men, I'd love to be able to say was true, but the reality was that when we did end up in bed, I didn't perform well. I was nervous, excited, pissed, and struggled to get a hard-on.

We did see each other for a short time, and eventually, this was one of the reasons that my marriage to Sandra broke up. So some good did come out of it. I don't know how much the newspaper paid Estelle for her story, and I don't know what happened to her. What I do know is that I was very unhappy at that time. My marriage wasn't good, and I did some stupid things. At least I am now happier than I've ever been. I am married to Helen, have two beautiful children with her, and life couldn't be better.

Over the years, I have done all sorts of strange jobs, and been booked as the face to launch a lottery-style venture. This was a long time before The National Lottery started. It was an idea put together by a group of M.P.'s who seemed to have seen a gap in the market. The launch was to be in Glasgow, but I was working in Cheltenham the night before, so they arranged for a small plane to fly me up there. I arrived at the small airstrip between Cheltenham and Gloucester very early in the morning. It was still dark, and I was sitting in a small room when this small bloke walked in. "Mr. Vasey?" he said. I said that I was, and he asked me to follow him. We walked across the grass, and up to a small propeller-driven plane. He opened the door and asked me to get in. It only had four seats and I wasn't impressed. The small man climbed into the pilot's seat and handed me a thick blanket, "I'm sorry" he said, "The heater doesn't work." Now, I'm not a good flyer at the best of times, so I was now thinking about Buddy Holly and Glenn Miller. He then handed me a pair of headphones and told me that they would drown out the noise of the engines! Then, just to really upset me, he informed me that we would be flying at a height of 4,000 ft. We took off and started the journey, and, when I eventually opened my eyes, the view was stunning. We flew over the Lake District, which makes you realise what a beautiful country we live in.

We arrived in Glasgow and I was taken to one of the most exclusive hotels in the city. It was called 1, The Terrace. Miss World was waiting there for me. They had hired her as well, and I for one wasn't complaining. She looked and smelled gorgeous, and was a lovely girl. The day went well, and the TV adverts followed. Ultimately, the venture fizzled out, and The National Lottery became massive. If you're wondering, I travelled home on the train, fuck them little Lego-type planes.

In this business, you have great days when you are treated like a star and spend the day with Miss World, but you always come down to earth with a bump. A few days after the Glasgow event, I had to travel to Barnstaple. It took forever to get there because the traffic was particularly bad, and it is such a long way from Teesside. When you left the M5, at that time, it was a long drive to Barnstaple on poor country roads. So when I arrived at the theatre, I was pretty pissed off. The theatre seemed so small, and looked like it only held about 12 people. The manager introduced himself and proceeded to tell me about all the stars that had appeared there. I have to admit that I hadn't heard of any of them.

The next day, we had to travel another six hours in the car to the next gig. These are the times that you feel like giving up. Sitting in a car for that long is a complete waste of human life, especially if they don't laugh when you get there. I used to say that I could tell you how many cats' eyes were on the M1, because I had travelled up and down it so many times. When you use motorways as much as I do, you realise what death-traps they are, especially in thick fog.

Travelling south on the M1 one day, we were doing about 70mph, when the fog came down. John York was my driver at the time, and we slowed down and pulled into the inside lane with the other sensible drivers. As we did this, a bank of red lights appeared in front of us, but vehicles were still flying past us in the other lanes. I said, "look at those fucking idiots, someone's going to get hurt." Of course, seconds later, BANG, BANG, BANG as cars and trucks ploughed into other cars and trucks, it was carnage. We pulled onto the hard shoulder and got out of the car where you really couldn't see your hand in front of you. I could hear a cry for help coming from a large truck's cab. I made my way over to where the voice was coming from and found the driver stuck underneath the engine, which had been forced into the cab. I have never felt so useless in my life; I didn't know what to do. I did have a phone in my car, which was a new thing in those days, so I called 999. The operator told me that they were aware of the situation, and Police, Fire Brigade and Ambulances were on the way. I returned to the truck to try and reassure the driver. I told him to hang on in there as help was on its way. Very soon, the emergency services arrived. I stayed with the driver and kept talking to him. Suddenly I was aware that someone was stood behind me. It was a policeman and he asked me who I was. I told him and he said, "well get back in your fucking car and don't move." Looking back, I realise that he was taking charge of the situation quickly and was doing what he was trained for. I did as I was told.

The next day, the headlines in the daily papers read, "Four car drivers and one truck driver killed in M1 smash." I just knew that it was the poor guy I had tried to help. I have to admit that as big as I am, I did shed a few tears over that bloke. To this day, I am always very wary of fog on the roads, and if I am being driven, I always insist that we slow down. Please, if you take one thing away from reading this book, let it be this story, and remember to slow down in fog.

# Mick Miller

When I first started doing shows at The South Pier in Blackpool, I would do a late show. Blackpool was buzzing, and had "Summer Shows" on at The South, Central and North Pier Theatres as well as those at The Opera House, Grand Theatre and The Pleasure Beach, and many of the stars would meet up for a drink after they had finished. There was a "Late Bar" at The Viking Hotel near The South Pier, and it was a great place to relax and unwind.

Mick Miller, the bald comedian with the long hair, if that makes sense, was one of the acts on the earlier show. In my opinion, he is one of the funniest comedians in the country, and I really enjoyed watching him work. We became friends, and I would regularly go to his house for his near-legendary barbecues. They were great fun on a Sunday afternoon, but I couldn't drink, because I had to work on the evening. Loads of people would be there, and everyone would congregate in "Miller's Bar," which Mick had created at his home for anyone to come round and have a natter. I've had some great times in there.

In January/February 1990, Mick toured in Australia and was due back in the UK for his fortieth birthday. His partner, Wendy, had organised a surprise birthday party for him at The Queens Hotel in Blackpool. All of his family and friends were there, and the idea was for us all to hide in the function room. Wendy had arranged it so that Mick thought he was going there to do a gig. He was knackered from his flights from Australia, but he managed to drag himself there.

I was hiding in the room with Pete Richardson, and we had all been given "Max Wall" style wigs, which were bald on the top and had long hair down the sides. We all put them on to look like Mick, and waited in silence. But you know how it is when you're supposed to keep quiet; everything becomes very funny. As I looked around the room, all I could see was the bald wigs with the long hair. So I said, "How the fuck are we going to know which is him?" Everyone laughed, and we were all told to keep quiet. I was getting bored with waiting, so I decided to make sure he would recognise me by writing, "Fuck Off" on my bald wig. Suddenly, the door opened, and Mick came into the dark room looking puzzled because he was expecting to be doing a gig. Somebody turned the lights on, and we all jumped up and sang "Happy Birthday To You." He was quite shocked and, as he looked around the room at all these people in the bald wigs, it was difficult to tell who was who, but he took one look at me and said, "Hello Chubbs." I think the "Fuck Off" had given me away!

Mick and I have remained good friends, and when Steve Cowper had his big fall out with George and Michael Forster, which resulted in him leaving the show, Mick called him up. He asked Steve if he wanted to work for him. Steve agreed, and now looks after all of Mick's work for him.

# Club Owners

Some of the cabaret club owners can be very funny. I suppose that they have picked it up from all the comedians that they have booked over the years. One of the funniest was Derek Smith, the owner of The Frontier Club in Batley, West Yorkshire. The venue had previously been the famous Batley Variety Club, and Derek had been the manager and had eventually bought the club.

In a previous incarnation, Derek had been a singer and piano player, so he was very used to being the centre of attention, and boy did he enjoy being the centre of attention. I loved Derek, because he was so down to earth, and he just made me laugh. I used to do three nights on the trot at The Frontier, and was always looked after well. The dressing room had comfortable sofas, a TV and most importantly, a kettle, tea and coffee and biscuits. But on one occasion, when I arrived, there were no biscuits! So when Derek called into the dressing room to say hello, I jokingly asked if he was in financial difficulties. He said that of course he wasn't, and asked why I thought that. I said that I thought he was saving money by not putting biscuits in the dressing room, and he laughed. The next evening, I couldn't move in that room for biscuits. The cheeky bastard had gone to the local biscuit factory and bought loads and loads of packets to shut me up. There must have been a hundred packets of biscuits of every type in that room.

The club would be packed when I was there, and they used to sell seated tickets and standing tickets. The tables could seat four, six or eight people, and Derek had made sure that every seat had been sold. When they opened the doors, people with seated tickets were allowed into the club half an hour earlier than the standing tickets so as to find their seats. Derek would be on the private balcony where the sound and lighting desks were housed. He could see all the tables, and would direct everyone over the mic. His times on the mic became comedy gold. He would say things like, " Table 31, bunch up, you need to have two more people on that table." But that wasn't all he'd say. My favourite was, "Don't forget the Burger Bar is now open. It is situated to the left of the stage, and tonight they have Plain Burgers, Cheese Burgers, Chicken Burgers and Veggie Burgers. Why anyone would want a Veggie Burger, I don't know, we're meant to eat meat. But I suppose some people might be daft enough to be vegetarians!"

He also used to treat the customers as if they were thick. One of his announcements went, "If you want the toilets, they are at the front of the room at the left and right. Don't be coming into the foyer and asking us where they are; because we've got better things to do than tell you where they are again. Oh, and if you don't know what the foyer is, it's the main entrance!" He was funny, but he could handle himself too and wasn't afraid of anybody. Steve told me about the time that he was in the foyer (main entrance) getting ready to sell the merchandise after the show. The club's security had asked a bloke to leave because he wouldn't stop talking when I was onstage, and people around him couldn't hear me properly because of him. He had been asked to keep quiet several times, and finally told to leave. He wasn't happy about this, and was arguing with the head of security in the foyer. Derek stood to one side, and let the discussion go on for a short while, but the bloke wasn't going to go. Derek then calmly walked over and said, "OK, I've heard enough of your voice now, just fuck off out of the club." The bloke then started to get angry and turned that anger towards Derek. He demanded to see the manager, as he wasn't going to be talked to like that. Derek then said, "You can't see the manager, now fuck off you thick cunt, and get out of the club and don't ever come back." The bloke repeated his request to see the manager as he was going to report Derek to him and would get him sacked." Derek then said, "You can't get me sacked, cos I own the fucking place, now fuck off." Steve said that the bloke's face was a picture as he left the club, and Derek turned to Steve and said, "You've just got to tell them sometimes. They can be a bit thick." This was Derek's idea of customer service, but it seemed to work for him.

There are many more stories about Derek, but I won't go into them. We became great friends, and when I won the "Comedian of The

Year" in 1990, they asked me whom I would like to present me with the award. There was only one person for the job, Derek Smith.

The awards night was at the Lakeside Country Club in Surrey, and the owner there was another showbiz legend, Bob Potter. He was a very shrewd man. The club was just part of his business empire and was built at the side of a lake. He also had a couple of hotels on the site, as well as others in different areas. Bob was one of the old school, his philosophy was to work hard, and he would always be in the club until it closed, and then would always be up and working at seven o'clock the next morning. I'm trying to be polite when I say he wasn't a young man, but he could run rings around some of his younger staff. Bob now owns the British Darts Organisation, and holds the TV rights as far as I know. He is an inspirational man.

I have to mention Kings Club in Great Barr near Birmingham. I used to work at this club regularly, and Tony, the owner, was one of the nicest guys you could wish to meet. He was very tall, and everyone referred to him as Big Tony. The club wasn't that big, but it had a great atmosphere. It was a great shame when the lease ran out, and it had to close. It was so sad to see it demolished.

Finally, there was George Savva, who I have mentioned before. He had known most of the big stars over the years, and had managed several clubs such as Blazers at Windsor and Caesars Palace at Luton. My favourite story that he told was when he was at Blazers. He had regular customers, and he knew them all by name. One night, a woman asked to see him as she had a complaint. She was sat on the small balcony area and wasn't happy. He met her in the foyer, and the woman said, "Mr. Savva, do I look like a Toby Jug tonight?" "Of course not, you look wonderful, I love your dress, and your hair is very nice tonight as well." She then said, "Well why have you put me on a fucking shelf!" You just can't answer that can you?

# The Rock Star

The north-east has produced so many great singers, and I have been privileged to know quite a few of them. David Coverdale of Deep Purple and Whitesnake fame was born in Saltburn-by-the Sea. Chris Rea is from Middlesbrough, and AC/DC front man, Brian Johnson was born in Dunston, Gateshead. I would bump into these guys when we were all gigging in bands around the north-east and still see them on different occasions.

Brian Johnson now lives a very different life in Florida, and tours the world with his band. He's hugely successful and very wealthy, but remains as down to earth as he was all those years ago. I was working at The Lakeside Country Club for a couple of nights, when there was a knock on my dressing room door. I shouted, "Come in," and when the door opened, Brian was stood there with his mate. They had just flown in to the UK for some gigs and found out that I was working nearby, so he decided to surprise me. He certainly did that, and we gave each other a big hug and started chatting about how we were and what we were doing. It was great to see him again.

After the show, I had arranged to go out for a curry with the lads on my crew, so I invited Brian and his mate along too. The restaurant was in the small town near the club, and was a couple of miles away, so we jumped in the cars and headed off. I introduced Brian and his mate to the lads. The only person who wasn't there was Arran, my sound guy. He had opted to stay back at the venue to sort out a small problem with the sound rig, and would follow us down to the restaurant as soon as possible. He had asked Steve to order his food and drinks for him to save time.

As soon as our table was ready, we all sat down. I sat opposite Brian so we could have a good chat over the meal, and Steve sat to Brian's left-hand side, but he left a space between them. He ordered Arran's meal and a pint of lager, which he placed in the vacant space. Arran arrived about ten minutes later and Steve called him over to the seat that he had saved. Arran took a large gulp of his lager as he settled down. He thanked Steve for sorting out the drink and ordering his food. He looked over to me and said how good he thought the show had been that night. He turned and looked at Brian, then turned to Steve, then looked back at Brian. Then he went a bit pale and leant over to Steve and whispered, "That's Brian Johnson from AC/DC!" Steve smiled and said that it was. You see, unbeknown to me, Arran was a huge AC/DC fan, but Steve knew this, and made sure Arran would get to sit next to his hero. His face was a picture, but he introduced himself and Brian started chatting to him as if they were long-lost friends. Like I said earlier, he is so down-to-earth, and is great company. Arran was over the moon.

Time has moved on, and both Steve and Arran have carried on working in show business. Steve now works with Mick Miller (as I mentioned earlier), who is one of my favorite comedians. Arran now owns a very successful sound hire company and still supplies the sound for my shows. They also supply the sound and production for Joe Longthorne. Coincidentally, Mick Miller has been working on that show as Joe's special guest star. Arran was mixing the show, and Steve was there with Mick. They got talking over an after-show pint, when somebody asked Arran about all the people he had met over the years. They asked him if he ever got star-struck, and Arran's reply was, "Just once, it was when I met my hero, Brian Johnson. He was so nice, and it was a pleasure to be in his company." I just thought that was such a nice story to tell, because some big stars become the most obnoxious people you could ever wish to meet. So it's nice to know that Brian has managed to keep it real and not let it all go to his head.

# Banger, Blazers & Bullshit

"**B**lazers" was a well-known club in Windsor, and it was a place that we did quite regularly. It was quite big, and hosted evenings with most of the big stars of the day. Freddie Starr and Danny La Rue would do a week at a time there. I would do two nights, and the place would be packed. The venue loved having me there because they would make a fortune on the bar sales. Some nights, I would go on stage and it was just a case of crowd control rather than doing a proper show.

One night, it was particularly bad, and I was getting really pissed off by a table full of blokes near the front of the stage. They were downing champagne as if it was going out of business, and they were getting louder and louder. Every time they ordered a new round of drinks, they had an argument over who was paying. Eventually, after telling them to shut up several times, I had had enough. I decided that I wasn't going to carry on with this disruption so near the stage as it was very off-putting. I walked off, and called "Banger" to the dressing room. He had been running all around the room trying to keep some sort of order. I told him that the table at the front had to be ejected, or I wouldn't go back on. So, he went back into the room and chucked them out. You could hear the rest of the audience cheer as they were led out; they really had been spoiling it for everyone. When I walked back on to the stage, a huge round of applause greeted me. I said, "I'm sorry about those arseholes, but they were spoiling it for all of you," and again the audience cheered. I was then able get on with the show. This time I could do my act, and I really enjoyed the rest of that show.

The next day, I had been into London to do some shopping. Banger had been with me and when we got back to our hotel the receptionist told us that two men had been looking for us. I thought no more about it until we arrived at the club. As we walked in, the manager asked to see Banger. George and Steve, who was my tour manager at the time, went with Banger to an office. I went to my dressing room.

After a while, Banger came backstage looking quite shaken up. I asked him what had happened, so he told me. I was quite shocked to hear that the club's owners had not been happy that their customers had been ejected from their club, and had brought in someone to "Have a word" about it. Banger told me what had happened in the office and I could hardly believe what he told me. As they had walked into the room one very large gentleman and one smaller man greeted them. The smaller one was wearing a smart pinstriped suit, which was pulled slightly open revealing what looked like a real handgun. The bigger man opened up by saying that he had been brought in to let us know that nobody threw people out of the club except himself. George had then started to answer him back, and was getting quite aggressive, but Banger had told him to keep quiet, as he was pretty sure he knew who this bloke was. Sure enough, the gorilla of a man then said, "Do you know who I am?" Banger replied, "I think so." "They call me The Guv'nor" was the reply. Banger was right; this was the legendary Lenny McLean. He was known as the toughest man in Britain. He was a bare-knuckle boxing champion, and a genuine hard bastard.

Banger admitted to me that he was actually quite worried that George would spout off to this man, and would end up in a bloody heap in the corner. You only have to look at videos of Lenny McLean on You Tube to see what he was like, to know that this was a distinct possibility. So he tried to keep things calm and explained that by throwing one table full of blokes out, he had made sure that everyone else had had a great night. If they had been allowed to stay and carried on like they had been, then the show would have stopped and they would have had a much bigger problem. Apparently, the tension in that office was scary and Banger had a brainwave. He remembered that Lenny was the head doorman at The Hippodrome nightclub in London, and when Lenny again said that he still shouldn't have thrown them out, and "We've got a problem with each other," Banger used his trump card. He said, "Lenny, I think we do have a problem, because if you want to kick off with me, there's a certain Glaswegian who lives in the Midlands, who won't be happy with you." Lenny thought for a second and said, "Are you Banger-Walsh, the ex wrestler?" Banger said, "Yes," and the atmosphere changed. You see, the owner of The Hippodrome also owned a string of clubs throughout the country, and Banger ran all of the doors for him in the Midlands area. Basically, they worked for the same man. Lenny then said, "Ok, I've heard all about you and I understand why you chucked them out, but I've been paid to frighten you, so if anyone asks, I've had a strong word with you." Banger agreed and they shook hands. This was a great example of diplomacy working in a difficult situation.

Over the years, Banger has told this story many times, but he tells me that if Lenny had decided to "kick off," he would have easily left Banger for dead. I can't exaggerate how scary this man was, and if you do look him up on YouTube, have a look at him in action in the ring with a fighter called Roy Shaw, and don't blink because you might miss it!

You can also see Tony "Banger" Walsh in action on You Tube in a tag-team wrestling match. He was partnered with "Rollerball Rocco" against Big Daddy and the unfortunately named black wrestler, "Kid Chocolate." We all know how wrestling is a "form of entertainment" but those guys had to be fit to do it. Banger would be on ITV's "World of Sport" most weeks, but I don't recall him ever winning. He was a baddie, and baddies never won. But he was no mug; once, in Leicester, I saw him lift a six-foot bloke off the ground by the throat to tell him to calm down. I also remember the time at Preston Guild Hall when a member of the audience was causing trouble. Banger went over and the idiot pulled a knife out and waved it at him. In those situations, a good security man just deals with it without thinking. Banger grabbed the bloke's wrist pulling his arm behind his back, but as the bloke fought back, he tried to stab Banger. So, in defence, he took control of the situation and broke the guy's arm. The police were called and the knifeman was taken away. I don't think he would have been writing any letters over the next few weeks!

You can tell that Banger was very loyal to me, and we became great friends. In fact, when I was diagnosed with throat cancer, he got in his car and drove up from Coventry just to offer me his support. He's a lovely guy, and would do anything for anyone. When the stunt man, Eddie Kidd, had his accident, Banger looked after him for ages. Recently, when Eddie got married, Banger was his Best Man.

Once, I had Banger staying at my house for a few days, and in many ways he's the perfect guest, but he could be quite clumsy. This was when I was still with Sandra and living at Sunnycross House. We had quite a narrow staircase, and as he went upstairs he knocked every one of the decorative plates off the wall. When he reached the top, he didn't even realise that he had done it!

On the road, we were all up for a laugh, and when I was in a market one day I saw a cheap watch. It was covered with fake diamonds and was obviously meant to look like an expensive watch. Banger was with me as I paid £14 for it. We hatched a plan, Pete's birthday was coming up, and I knew that he loved nice watches. I wrapped it up and Banger altered the receipt to read £1400. I got Banger to give it to Pete and explain that I felt embarrassed giving him such an expensive gift. Banger revelled in it, and I'm sure he made up some more bits to the story. Pete opened the watch, and Banger made the most of it. He even gave Pete the receipt for insurance purposes. Pete was speechless, but ultimately suspicious. It didn't take long for him to work out that this was actually a cheap watch, so he decided to get his own back on Banger for the wind-up.

A few weeks passed, and Pete now felt that the time was right to get his own back. We were working at the South Pier in Blackpool, and Pete walked down to find Banger in the foyer of the theatre. "Come quick," he said. "Chubby's got into a fight at the front of the pier." Banger dropped everything and ran like mad, but of course, there was no fight. In fact, I wasn't even there. Banger's face was like a tomato and he was sweating like a bull's bollocks as he headed back to the foyer. Pete was waiting for him, and just held his arm up and pointed to his wrist, "Remember the watch!" was all he said, and to this day, that is the phrase we all use to point out that something is just a "wind-up."

# *Vanity*

Vanity is a funny thing, and different people have different ideas about their appearance. One day when I looked in the mirror, I noticed that I was starting to go bald. It bothered me, and I began wondering if I should wear a toupee. On reflection, I decided against that idea and instead, did some research into having a hair transplant. But when I found out how much that would cost, I decided against that as well. I then came across a product called, "Mane." It was something that you sprayed on to make the hair that you have look thicker. I carefully followed the instructions, and I have to say, it did what it said on the tin. But, I also have to be honest and say I looked really stupid. All I could think of when I looked in the mirror was that it looked worse than that wig that Frankie Howerd used to wear.

By now, I have to admit that I was becoming obsessed and was willing to try anything. Eventually I found a specialist in Manchester, who had perfected a new technique. He took hair, which still grew, from the back of the head and then weaved it in to the thinning hair on the top. It took a while to do, but the result was amazing. I looked in the mirror and, to coin a phrase, I couldn't see the join.

I left the clinic and walked back to where I had parked the car. It was a warm sunny day, and the hotter it became, the more my head itched. The more it itched, the more I scratched and people kept looking at me scratching my head; they must have thought I had nits. But I convinced myself that it must have looked good, because nobody had actually recognised me. But as I approached my car, this bloke shouted over to me, "Now then Chubby, what the fuck is that you've got on your head?" Well, that was it; I went home, got the scissors out and started to cut it out. I couldn't stand the itching any more, and that bloke's comment had been the final straw.

As I hacked away with the scissors, my head was bleeding. I'd spent a fortune on my hair, and now here I was trying to get rid of it. Like I said, vanity is a funny thing, and in this case, quite painful.

Fucking wig

# *Cheltenham*

We had been working away for a 10-day run, which finished with a "Sold Out" gig at Cheltenham Town Hall. It was in the run-up to Christmas, and we had been doing extremely well on the merchandise sales. In those days, it was mainly cassette tapes, and I had just brought out a new one. So, with a pocket full of cash, I decided to do a bit of Christmas shopping and Cheltenham has some very classy shops, so it was the ideal place to get some nice presents.

As usual, we checked out of the hotel after breakfast, and headed to the venue to park. Pete drove my car and Steve followed in the van. After parking, we all went into the town. Now, as the lads will tell you, I do know how to shop! I like to buy nice things for those people close to me. Cheltenham town centre is like a treasure trove to me.

We were all dressed as you would be for travelling and working, Track suit bottoms and sweat shirts, and we set off on a Christmas shopping trip. Pete and Steve were getting a few things, but I was on a roll. After a while, we found a department store, which had everything. The lads were helping me carry the bags of stuff I had bought, and I kept seeing more things to buy. Eventually, I made my way to the till to pay. I pulled out a "wad" of cash, and paid the snooty woman at the till. On leaving the store, Pete said how snobby the shop was, and how the staff were looking at us as if we'd trodden in something!

It was nearly two o'clock, and I had nearly finished my shopping, so we were heading back to the venue, where I was going to put my feet up in the dressing room. On the way, we passed a clothes shop, and in the window, was an outfit that I knew my wife would love. I said to the lads, "I'm just going to pop in here to see if they had it in her size."

They decided to wait outside and sit on a bench. I went in, and spoke to a sales assistant. She helped me to get the outfit and some accessories, so I was a bit longer than I expected. When I left the shop, Pete and Steve were nowhere to be seen. I couldn't believe that they'd just leave without saying anything, but they had definitely gone. So I made my way back to the venue and hoped that they would be there, with a nice hot mug of tea for me, but they were nowhere to be seen. So I made myself a cuppa and sat down.

It must have been half an hour later when Steve came into the dressing room with a woman. I looked up, and my first reaction was to say, "Where the fuck did you get to?" The woman looked a bit shocked, and Steve said, "Roy, I've been arrested, and this is a policewoman who needs you to confirm my name." I looked at her, then at Steve, then back at her. I just laughed; I thought it was a wind-up. Then, she spoke, and explained that she was a plain-clothes police officer, and that Steve had been arrested, but they now thought that there was no reason to hold him, and if I could identify him, he would be "de-arrested." Now, to this day, I wish I'd said, "I have never seen this man before." It would have been funny. But somehow, the situation seemed quite serious, so I told them who he was. I remember saying to her, that Steve was as honest as the day is long, and, as a joke, said that if they had arrested my other mate, Pete, they might have found a stolen bike down each trouser leg! At this point, Pete walked around the corner with all the shopping bags, and said, "I've just been arrested!" I fell about laughing.

When we finally got an explanation from the police, they told us that a sales assistant from a large store had reported us to them. The reason? We had been buying things in the shop, and appeared to have a lot of money, but she didn't think we looked like the type of people to have money; we didn't look like "Cheltenham" people. So the police were mobilised, and managed to catch Pete and Steve, and arrested them on "suspicion of being in possession of counterfeit currency."

Looking back, it was funny, but it made me very wary of spending money in Cheltenham.

# First Time in Australia

I arrived in Sydney, full of expectations. I had travelled to the other side of the world, and was ready to get to work. The first gig turned out to be a small comedy club just under Sydney Harbour Bridge. The dressing room was very well-equipped; it had everything you could possibly need, if you were a chef! Yes, I had to get changed in the kitchen area. That was bad enough, but, to make it worse, all the chefs were Chinese, and didn't appreciate me getting in their way. They seemed to have learned one English phrase, which was "Move your arse out of way!" Cheeky bastards.

Anyway, I managed to get ready, and made my way to the stage. I had written some nice lines about travelling to Australia etc. but I couldn't get them out. The audience was just shouting abuse at me, and I was using every answer that I had. They were shouting, "You Fat Pommy Bastard," and I was calling them a bunch of deported criminals. I managed to do some sort of a show, and they loved it I got a standing ovation. But I was thinking that if this is what the Australians are going to be like, I'm getting the first plane home.

After the show, it was explained to me that they have a philosophy, and that is that you only have one life, so enjoy it, and they were just enjoying it. I thought about this, and when we went to Manley Beach the next day, it clicked, and suddenly I understood. It was the weekend, and whole families were on the beach together. They had crates of beer and lots of food. The younger ones were in the sea, surfing. The girls were sunbathing, and everyone was having fun. The atmosphere was fantastic. I mean, there was wall-to-wall pussy, and fit, young, tanned, good-looking lads drooling at them just like a dog in a butcher's shop.

We, on the other hand, looked like fish out of water, with our white legs, black socks and in my case, a "small" belly! We only needed Union Jack shirts to complete the "Brit Abroad" look. You see, we were fresh off the plane from a cold UK winter, and looked like we had just come off the night shift at the flour factory, we really were that white.

We decided to call into a bar for a drink, and there were scantily clad, stunning women everywhere. Every one of them could have been Miss World. It was at this point that I realised I was getting old, but it didn't stop me dreaming. I now understood the Aussie lifestyle, and thought that I could get used to it, so I decided to stick it out for another couple of weeks. I now love Australia and am always happy to work over there.

I am what is generally known as a "fair weather" golfer, and Australia has its fair share of fair weather. They also have some fabulous golf courses, so we asked around and found somewhere to play. I was quite looking forward to the game until I noticed a sign near the first tee. "WARNING," it read, "DO NOT ATTEMPT TO RETRIEVE LOST BALLS FROM THE ROUGH. DANGER FROM CROCODILES AND POISONOUS SNAKES." I had to ask if it was a joke, but it wasn't. I couldn't believe it.

Anyway, we started our game, carefully staying away from the rough! As we rounded a corner to the fourth tee, a uniquely Australian creature came into view. It was my first sighting of a kangaroo, and everyone does the same thing. Firstly, you look it up and down, then you say, "Fucking Hell, look at the size of its bollocks!" Then you phone home to tell everyone you've just seen your first kangaroo, and that it has an enormous pair of bollocks. It wasn't on its own, there were whole families of them on this fairway, and the big male ones just looked at you, as if to say, "I'm not moving for anything, so if you want some, come and get it." It is a truly amazing sight.

After we had finished, we had a "tinny" in the clubhouse, and then went back into Sydney. I had heard about the famous "Paddy's Market" and I wanted to go shopping there. They had everything, and if they didn't, it wasn't worth buying. I had a ball, and bought loads of stuff. In fact I had to buy another suitcase just to fit all my purchases in. I ended up sending this case home by courier, as I would have had too much luggage to get on the plane.

The second gig was at a rugby club, and I had been told not to think that it would be like the old British rugby clubs that I used to do in the early days. Sure enough, when we got there, it was nothing like them. It was massive and had shops, bars, restaurants, a gym and even a bowling alley. The cabaret room was quite big, and very well-equipped with great sound and lighting. I asked what sort of acts they normally had on here, and was told that the previous night, Leo Sayer had performed, and the following night The Searchers were on. I felt like I was in good company.

After the rowdy first show at the comedy club, I was still a bit apprehensive, but I needn't have worried. The audience was fantastic, and very well-behaved. Whilst I was on stage, a guy walked back from the bar with a tray of drinks. There were six pints of lager on it, and he made his way to the front of the stage. "Here you go Chubby, have a drink with us." So, I bent down, took a pint and said "Thank you mate, I'll enjoy it." The guy looked up at me and said, "Chubby, they're all for you!" Quick as a flash, I said, "Well I like a drink, but I don't need a fucking bath!" This was another example of Aussie mentality. If I were a young man with no ties, I'd be out there

# My Birthday in Hong Kong

My second "world tour" had been planned, and I was looking forward to it. We were to play Hong Kong, New Zealand, Australia and Bahrain. Universal Film and Video were involved and we would be filming shows and documentary footage in Australia. We had the luxury of "Round The World" business class flight tickets, and the first flight was on Cathay Pacific Airlines to Hong Kong. All the crew was included in the business class deal, so we were all in a great mood.

We arrived in Hong Kong and went straight to the hotel. The traffic was horrendous and as we were driven down the road to the hotel, we were aware that people were walking faster than us, and nearly everyone had a mobile phone permanently to their ear. This was one hell of a busy city!

Finally, we arrived at the hotel and I went to my room to relax. It was my birthday, and we had the night off. The crew went to check out the venue and returned later. Arran, who was my sound engineer at the time, was very impressed with the sound equipment that they had at the venue, and couldn't get over the fact that they had a complete spare system just sat in a room, just in case something went wrong with the first.

We had all arranged to meet up in the hotel bar at 7.00pm so we could decide what to do for the evening. I was keen to have a meal with everyone to celebrate my birthday, so I said to Steve, "Do you think we could find a decent Chinese restaurant anywhere around here?" Steve just looked back at me, and said, "Roy, we're in China. What do you think?" It took a second for it to sink in; I hadn't even connected Hong Kong and China in my mind.

Michael Forster had arranged to meet one of his friends who now worked in Hong Kong as a lawyer. So, when he arrived, I asked if he knew of a good place to eat. He asked if we wanted a tourist Chinese meal, or a proper one. "What's the difference?" I asked. He said that you could go to the main tourist areas and find a restaurant with a nice décor and waiters in authentic Chinese dress, or you can go to the places the locals eat. We decided on the proper place, where the locals ate, so he took us to a place in the back streets. It was only small, and we just about took over the whole restaurant. The lawyer ordered everything in fluent Cantonese (or whatever the correct language was), and I have to say that everything was consumed as if it was the Last Supper. It was one of the best Chinese meals I have ever tasted. However, I stopped asking what things were after the pigeon (complete with head) was brought to the table. Everyone said how much they had enjoyed the meal, sang "Happy Birthday" to me, and it was time to leave.

On the way back to the hotel, our new lawyer friend suggested that we have a look at the midnight market. I was up for it, so off we went. It was just like many other markets around the world, but it was midnight! As we walked through, I noticed a small man sat cross-legged at his stall, selling sex aids. He saw me looking, and beckoned me over. I was up for a laugh, and picked up a massive dildo, and we were all laughing. The stallholder was a bit of a character, but spoke no English, so we communicated by sign language. He was laughing at me waving the dildo around, and I was playing to the crowd. He then produced a small bottle and showed it to me. He then tried to explain what it was for, by making the universal sign for a hard-on, with his forearm and clenched fist. I couldn't resist it, so I bought it, along with the dildo and some other stuff just for the laugh. Then went back to the hotel (on my own!) and went to bed.

The next day was the day of the gig, and it was uneventful, but good. I went straight back to the hotel, and we flew to New Zealand the next morning. The flight went via Singapore, where we stopped to refuel. Shep, my lighting guy, was quite emotional, as he had been born in Singapore, but left (with his parents) soon after. He had never been back since, so this would be his homecoming. We landed, and would have to leave the plane whilst it was refueled. This would be the first time he had stood on Singapore soil since he left all those years ago, and it obviously meant a lot to him. We would only be going into a transit lounge, but it was still a big deal to him. Ritchie had a plan; he disappeared for a while, and then came back. When we were called to disembark, we went to the aircraft door to head to the transit lounge. But, one of the cabin crew pulled Shep to one side. Ritchie had asked if he could actually get on to the ground, so he would have actually been on Singapore soil. They had arranged it, and he was allowed down some steps, and outside. When he looked up, we were all watching and taking video footage for him. He was obviously moved, but still managed to play up for the camera by kneeling down and kissing the ground. We all took the piss, but he was happy and bought everyone some proper Singapore beer in the bar.

We arrived in New Zealand, and waited in the baggage reclaim area. Everyone had a job to do, and the crew retrieved our luggage, which included golf clubs, personal suitcases, equipment for the show and, of course, my patchwork suits etc. All in all, there was 36 pieces of luggage. Everything used for the show had to have a customs "Carnet" form stamped on entry and exit from every country, and Arran had the responsibility for this. It included a radio mic system that fitted in to my flying hat, mini disc player, and my personal hand-held mics. But we also had to declare my stage props, which included the false cock (and a spare) that I use in my "Full Monty" routine. We thought it was funny how they had been declared on the customs form as, "False Male Genitalia x 2"

Arran went off to the customs point, Steve, Ritchie and Shep loaded up a big trolley with the luggage, and impatient George decided to grab the trolley with the golf clubs on and head off through the Nothing to Declare exit. As he moved forward, an official, who told him to follow the signs for contaminated goods, met him. Apparently, New Zealand is very protective about their environment, and is very keen not to allow any foreign soil or vegetation into the country. The clubs and golf shoes may be contaminated, and must be checked and sterilised. So, not only was George held up whilst this was done, he was also charged a fee for the cleaning/sterilisation. We thought it was quite funny, but George wasn't laughing, he'd only been in the country for 5 minutes, and it had cost him nearly $100. He said, "At least it was only golf clubs and shoes, nothing to be embarrassed about." "You think so?" I asked. He looked puzzled. So I put him out of his misery and told him. "Do you remember that market in Hong Kong?" He said he did "Well, you know all those sex aids I bought, they're all in my golf bag. They must have seen them when they checked the bags." George went red, "I wondered why they were looking at me like that!" he said.

For the rest of the tour, we found our way through customs without incident until we left Australia. As usual, Arran had to get the customs form stamped. Usually, it's just a formality, although they can ask to inspect the goods. Nobody had bothered throughout the tour, and it only ever took a few minutes. However, this time, the woman customs officer checked the form and laughed out loud. She then said that she had done this job for years, and had never had a form that stated "False Male Genitalia x 2" and she just had to see them. The other customs officers gathered around whilst Arran had to produce the false cocks for them all to have a good laugh at. At least some customs officials have a sense of humour.

The end of this story happens when I got home. I had been back a week, when I remembered the little bottle of liquid that I had bought in Hong Kong. I though I'd give it a try, so I dug it out and rubbed it in. I waited expectantly, but nothing happened. By the next morning, my cock felt like it was burning. There was a rash on it and it was very painful. I wanted to get a flight back to Hong Kong, go back to that market and make him rub it into his cock to see how he liked it. I had a shower, and rubbed some cream in. After a couple of days, the rash had gone, and it didn't hurt any more. I was determined to find out what this stuff was, so when I was going to my favourite Chinese restaurant in Middlesbrough, I took it with me. I knew the staff well, and they knew me, so it was easy to ask for a translation of the label. I explained what I had done and what had happened, and that I wanted to know why. The manager put his glasses on and read it carefully. "You dozy bastard" he said. "Yes, it does give the same effect as Viagra, but you don't rub it in, you put three drops in half a pint of water, then you drink it!" It turned out that it was a highly concentrated liquid, so no wonder I had a sore cock.

# *Australia*

I have been lucky enough to work all over the world, and Australia has to be one of the best places to be. I knew that I would be performing to mainly "expats," but they all seem to embrace the Aussie lifestyle, and because of this, they take on the laid-back attitude. It's a fantastic country.

I suppose we all have our favourite stories, and I know that this one is Steve's. We were finishing the Australian leg of a world tour, and had four nights in a theatre in Perth. For those of you who don't know, Perth is a very long way from anywhere. In fact, I was told it is closer to Singapore than Sydney. It's a lovely city. It's very clean, and the people are so nice, but it is very insular. The promoter had booked us into a nice hotel, but all the crew asked if we could stop at the smaller hotel that we had stopped in the previous year. It was cheaper, and a bit more out of the way. But the real reason became clear about 30 seconds after checking in. They all rushed up to their rooms, opened their luggage and ran like hell to the lift. It turned out that the first one to the basement got to the laundry room first, and got first use of the complementary washing machine! Can you imagine what their working clothes must have been like after a couple of weeks on the road? I think that the clothes might have walked to the laundry room on their own. I had it sussed; I just bought new clothes as we went on.

Anyway, back to the story. When you tour in Australia, you have to have Australian content on the show, which is fair enough. But, when you're touring Australia, you have to fly everywhere, which gets expensive. So the promoter decided to use local acts for the support spot. Quite honestly, some were OK, and some were not that good.

When we arrived in Perth, the crew was setting up for the show, but there was no sign of the support act. Ritchie and Shep were ready to focus the lighting, and needed to know where the band would be positioned. So the promoter phoned them. They were all still at work, and said that they would be there in time for the show, which wasn't exactly professional, but we had to live with it. They said that they would fax a stage plan over to us, so we would be able to set the lighting. The lads got the fax and burst out laughing. It showed piano, drums and double bass. It was obvious that they were a Jazz Band! There's nothing wrong with that, but it's just not the type of act to put on as a support act on one of my shows. I don't think my audiences would appreciate Jazz.

Eventually, they arrived, set up their gear, and only had time for a very quick sound check. They were quite good, but we could see what was going to happen. So we asked if they knew what they had let themselves in for. The girl singer was the one in charge, and she seemed annoyed that we had even questioned their credentials. She informed us that they were, "The best band in Perth," and that they were the band that did all the "Gentlemen's Evenings" in all the hotels in Perth. They were simply the perfect choice as they were so good. They were so full of themselves that they didn't want to listen to us. So we let them get ready, and head to the stage for the show.

The musicians arrived on-stage first. They were dressed in dinner suits with bow ties. Then the girl singer arrived in a proper ball gown. It didn't look good for them, but they were still oblivious to what was about to happen. Steve did an off-stage announcement to introduce them, the curtains opened, and the band started playing some standard Jazz song. Seconds later, the girl stepped out from the wings. She had reached the point of no return; she was on-stage and had about twenty feet to walk to the microphone at the centre of the stage. There was no turning back. The audience had smelt blood, and began shouting insults. Then, there seemed to be a lull in the noise, the girl looked up and smiled at the audience, and at that point, one lone voice shouted out, "Oi, Sheila, show us your flange piece!" The girl stumbled and looked defeated before singing a note. They did a very short set, left the stage and complained about the audience. They refused to come back for the other three shows, so we had to get special permission to do them without any Australian content. I just had to do a longer show. It was the best-timed heckle I have ever heard, and one of the funniest.

# The Sport of Kings

I like a bet on the horses, and when somebody said to me, that for the amount of money that I had spent on betting on them, I could have bought one, it got me thinking, and I thought, why not, I can afford it, so I decided to look for a racehorse to buy. I approached Kevin Ryan, who is one of the best trainers in the north-east. He had a horse called "Razzaman" and it was for sale at thirty-five thousand guineas. I thought about it for a while, and with encouragement from Helen, I decided to go for it. We shook hands, and I became a racehorse owner.

Now, you have to know that the trouble with trainers is that they will tell you that he has a good chance of winning at a particular meeting, so you get all excited, and it comes in last. Then, when they don't tell you anything, the bastard thing goes and wins. So when he told me that it would be racing at Musselborough and that it stood a good chance because it was uphill to the finishing post, and he always came on strong at the end of a race, you guessed, it came nowhere. I mean, the only time it got to the rails was to lean on them. When it came over the finishing post, they gave the jockey the keys to the racecourse and asked him to lock up as everyone had gone home!

He was due to race at Catterick, which is quite close to where I live, so I decided to go. Everyone at the course knew me, and they were all putting money on my horse. Bugger me, the bloody thing won at 5/1. It was a fantastic day and I was over the moon. I was on a high and couldn't wait until his next race. I thought that now he had won, he must have turned the corner, and would now compete at a better level. The bastard thing came last again and I just couldn't understand it. I went over to him in the paddock and stood in front of him. I looked him straight in the eye and said, "I know a fucking good butcher who sells horse meat. Buck your ideas up!" The trainer saw this and pissed himself laughing. The thing is, I was getting a bit pissed off with being an owner. When I bought him, the trainer told me to expect to be paying around about £200 per week in costs, but when my first bill came, it was for £4000, so I was straight on to the phone. I asked why the bill was so much, and was told that there had been some extra expenditure. Apparently he had had his teeth done, got some new shoes and had its tongue strapped down. I said has it been to the hairdressers as well, and whilst we're on with this, what sort of shoes were they, Jimmy Choo's? I did have a few more wins and places with him, but I eventually sold him. It was a great experience and I might do it again one day.

Back in the sixties, I had a big win with a sixpence Yankee. I had picked four horses, and they all came in. "Await The Slates" (8/1), "Bo Normund" (6/4) "Jay Trump" (100/8) and another horse that I can't recall the name of. I won a few thousand pounds, which was worth a lot more in those days. I went straight to the Fairway Pub in Dormanstown and bought everybody a drink. Suddenly, everyone was drinking double brandies when 5 minutes before, they had been drinking pints of bitter. Who would ever have thought that I would one day be standing in the winner's enclosure as the owner of the winning horse. The stupid thing is that I would never have been able to do this if it wasn't for years of trekking around the world in a patchwork suit and a leather flying helmet. I owe a lot to being "Chubby Brown," and I never ever forget that.

# Personal Registration Numbers

Isn't it funny that we like to have personal registration plates. I don't know why that is, but lots of people get them. Many years ago, I bought the number RCB 250, and it has been on lots of my cars. It wasn't too expensive when I bought it, but if I were to sell it now, I'd make a good profit. Well, Pete Richardson has always had a wicked sense of humour, and if he smelled a rat, he was like a dog with a bone; he would never let it drop. So when he noticed that George Forster, my ex-manager, had a registration that included the letters GFJ, he wouldn't let it go. He kept asking George why he had GFJ, and not just GF. Was it because it was too expensive? George's answer was that the letters GFJ stood for George Forster Junior.

Years went by, and Pete kept mentioning George's number plate as a bit of a long-running joke. One day, he asked George what his father was called, and it turned out that his name was Tommy. Pete was in his element, "I thought he was called George," he said, but George said that it was definitely Tommy. Well that was it; Pete had him. "So your plate doesn't mean George Forster Junior then!" George, quick as a flash said, "Well you can't get GF as a plate because it's reserved for the Ministry of Defence. It stands for Ground Forces." Pete didn't believe him, and kept up the gag that it was because he was a bit "tight," and didn't want to pay the extra money for a two-letter plate. Of course, George denied this.

Months later, I was in London in a taxi with Pete and George, when an excited Pete pointed out a car with the registration number, GF 9. George knew he was now beaten, and he said, "OK, I wonder what it stands for." Pete then said, "Probably Greedy Fucker!" Oh how we laughed. George paid for all the meals at a restaurant that night.

Many years later, when I bought a new Lexus car, we were talking about number plates. Steve suggested that the number CHU 88Y would be a great number for me. I told him to look into it and see if it was for sale, and how much it would cost. I had been doing very well, and my video sales were great, so I thought I would treat myself if it were available.

Steve spoke to Danny Plummer, who was the Lexus salesman. Danny found out that the number had never been released, so he contacted DVLA to see about buying it. They said that they would release it for sale, but it would have to go to auction. So Steve and Danny offered to go and bid for the number.

Steve told me what happened when they got there. There was a buzz about this particular number plate, and everyone seemed quite excited. They got talking to a young bloke who asked them if they were there for any particular registration. They kept their cards close to their chests and said that they would see what came up. The bloke then told them that he had been left some money in a will, and was dabbling in number plate trading. He was there to get CHU 88Y, and he was prepared to spend up to £1500 to get it as he knew of a comedian called Chubby Brown, who would pay more than that to get it. He thought he could make "a few hundred quid" on the deal. Steve and Danny just smiled.

Eventually, the time for the auction came, and Steve called me so I could hear the bidding and tell him to carry on or stop. Of course, the bidding went way past that bloke's £1500 and soon reached £10,000. Steve and Danny hadn't even made a bid. I think every number plate dealer in the world had turned up to buy this plate to sell to me. It eventually sold for the ridiculous price of around £27,000 plus vat and other charges. There was no way that I was going to spend anything like that on a number plate for a car. I think that those dealers must have thought that I had more money than sense. In fact, that plate is still for sale and they are asking around £43,000 for it. I think I'll stick with RCB 250.

# The Car Park Incident

Unfortunately, fame brings unwanted attention, and I do seem to attract my fair share. I know that the industry I am in is all about wanting attention, and that's fine, but some people see me and other celebrities as a short cut to getting rich. Over the years, I have had people borrow money, only to disappear without paying me anything back. I've had people trying to con me out of money via financial investments, and I've had people selling stories to newspapers about me. It's just the way things are.

I've had people shout abuse at me and my family, and then when I react, they call the police and say that I've done something to them and they want compensation. I should know better now, but things still happen. The latest example of this was an incident in a Sainsbury's car park. I had popped out to get some shopping just like I had done hundreds of times before. I am not a "car nut" but I do like comfortable cars. Over the last few years, I have been using Lexus 4 wheel drive vehicles, which are fantastic. They have all the latest gadgets on them, and are very nice to drive.

On the day in question, I drove into the car park and looked for a space. I found one and proceeded to reverse the car into it. As I reversed, my parking sensors did their job and I positioned the car correctly in the parking space. I got out of the car and headed to the store, but was stopped in my tracks by a young woman who was screaming and bawling at me. She was accusing me of bumping into her grandmother's car, which was completely untrue. I told her that I hadn't done that, and that my car had a state-of-the art parking system which literally screams at you if you get too close to anything. She continued with her verbal assault, and then raised her hand and slapped me in the face, followed by hitting me twice in the chest. As she prepared to hit me again, I grabbed hold of her wrists and held them in self-defence. Then, and maybe I shouldn't have said this, but in the heat of the moment, I said, "If you're going to act like a man, I'll treat you like you're a man!" and I admit that I called her a "Fucking Scumbag." It was all over in a couple of minutes, and it left me fuming.

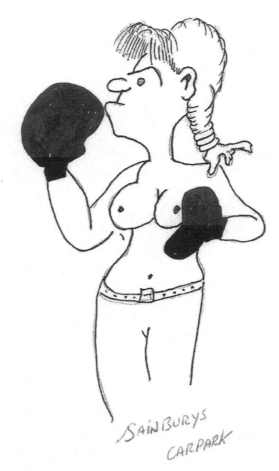

SAINBURYS
CARPARK

The next thing I knew about it all was when I got a call from the police. She had accused me of assaulting her. I couldn't believe it when I was charged over the incident. Not only would I have to attend court to answer these charges, which was bad enough, but the next day, the headline in The Sun Newspaper read, "18 STONE COMIC HITS 7 STONE GIRL." I was gutted; everyone in the country who reads that paper would believe that I had hit her! It seemed that I was already guilty in the eyes of the media.

Six and a half months later, the day of the trial arrived, and I had engaged the services of a legal team, which cost me several thousand pounds, and of course, I don't qualify for Legal Aid to defend myself, but the young woman who accused me did. In court that day, she looked like butter wouldn't melt in her mouth. She wore a pink tracksuit, and had even put her hair in bobtails to make her look younger and more vulnerable. She presented herself as a timid person who, since the incident was unable to go shopping or get on a bus. In fact, she had been so traumatised by this, she was now frightened of men, and couldn't go near any man for fear of being attacked. I think that might have been one lie too many, as this girl was now just over six months pregnant!

Local TV and national press were covering the case, and her solicitor was revelling in the limelight. It was like "Rumpole of The Old Bailey" in there. She opened her case by saying, "Soooooooo Mr. Vasey, there you are in Sainsbury's car park, with your big, shiny, new car, with all of its new technology. You could afford to shop anywhere, but you chose Sainsbury's in Middlesbrough." Then she laughed sarcastically. Well, I saw red and said, "Could I just stop you there. Would you be suggesting that I'm a cheapskate for shopping at Sainsbury's? Because you couldn't be any further from the truth." But she continued by saying, "Mr. Vasey, I put it to you that you ran across the car park and punched this girl in the face." I reminded her that if I had run across the car park and punched the girl in the face, she would have ended up in the shop, and not the fucking car park.

After the prosecution had tried to assassinate my character by bringing up things from my past, it was time for my solicitor to present my defence. I have to say, he was brilliant, and after referring to the prosecution's version of the events, he played the CCTV footage from the cameras in the car park. They plainly showed that I was telling the truth and that she had, in fact, assaulted me. I was acquitted and walked free from the court.

The next day, The Sun carried the news that I had been acquitted, but it was somewhere in the middle of the paper, and was just one paragraph with a small headline. Obviously that wasn't as good a story as if I had actually done it! I know that they have to sell newspapers, and it's all about the headlines, but I wish that they had covered my acquittal as much as they did the original story. I still get asked what the outcome of that trial was, and some people presume I actually did punch this woman. Now I'm not saying anything about her motives, but if they had got a guilty verdict, then a woman who was so traumatised that she couldn't go near a man, (but had got pregnant after the incident had already taken place) would have lodged a compensation claim. I have to ask myself if I weren't "Chubby Brown" would it have gone this far? Thank goodness for CCTV.

# *Australia 2011*

The latest Australian tour was good fun. We had great ticket sales and good reaction from the audiences. The downside was the seven flights in ten days. The first show was in Perth, and when I stood on-stage at some of the venues and saw up to two thousand smiling faces, I could tell that at least a thousand of them were British. The main give away was the football shirts that they proudly wore.

The second gig was in Sydney, and after a four and a half hour flight over from Perth; we arrived for the comedy festival. My show was due to start at 9.00pm after a performance by a Chinese comedian called Yin Lan Ken. He spoke good English and had a big screen showing pictures of jet engines and motorbikes. He wore a white coat and a yellow hard hat as he talked about the pictures on the screen. I didn't get it, and neither did the audience. They would politely laugh every so often, and because of this he thought he was doing well, so he kept going. He eventually came off at 9.00pm. His audience left, and mine came in. The venue was very efficient, and we didn't have to wait too long to get our show started. They were pumped up, and chanting "Chubby, Chubby, Chubby." I walked on and said, "I have to apologise for the late start, but we have just had a Chinese comedian on here before me. He should have been called "On Too Foo Kin Long." If he didn't have such squinty eyes, he would have seen the clock!" They loved it, and I had a great show.

The next show was in Melbourne, where we worked at The Crown Casino. After the show, I was talking to some people who had travelled in from the outback just to see my show. They had driven three and a half hours to get there, and then would have to drive the same to get back home. It really made me feel quite humble.

During the day, we walked around a market where we came across a café with a piano outside. Well, as you know, I enjoy playing the piano, and went across to have a look at it. There was a small sign stating that "The Ladies of The City" had donated it for anyone to play and enjoy. It didn't take much to convince me to get up and play. I bashed out a few tunes, and it caused quite a stir. I did attract a few people, but many of them hadn't got a clue as to whom I was.

Now, I have already mentioned about the Australian view on life. They just get on with it, and enjoy it to the full. They certainly aren't politically correct like we are over here. I mean, we have just produced the Oscar-winning film "The King's Speech," which is a heart-warming, sensitive portrayal of the King's battle against his chronic speech impediment. It was a triumph for the British film industry. But when I went to Australia in 2000, their big home-produced movie was called, "The Wog Boy." If you don't believe me, Google it!

I got talking to some Aussies about political correctness, and they couldn't believe that we have these rules and laws. They say it how they see it, and sod anyone else's feelings. Even the media over there uses terms that we aren't allowed to use. I remember seeing the cricket scores on the back page of a national paper. It simply said, "Australia wins, Pakis all out for 178." They do call a spade a spade, but that's probably another phrase that I'm not supposed to say! I've been called a racist many times, but all I do is say what I think, and I do try to make it humorous. I really don't think that I'm that different to a lot of other people, it's just that I was brought up in a different era. I don't hate anyone because of the colour of his or her skin or where they happened to be born. But I also don't like being told how to think and how to talk about anyone.

# *Why I Do This*

Everyone's heard the saying, "The show must go on." Well it's true, because when people have paid to see you perform; you feel that you can't let them down. I have walked on to stage with diarrhoea, cancer, bells palsy and a throat that was so sore, you'd think that I was a porn star that had had a cock down it for three weeks! You see, it's not about the money, and when you walk on to that stage and get laughs, it's like a drug that stops you from feeling ill. So, if I can walk and I can talk, I will definitely work.

I have been lucky enough to perform at the London Palladium, and when you stand in the wings waiting to go on to two thousand cheering people, the feeling that you get is indescribable. I have heard drug addicts describing the "buzz" that they get from taking their drug of choice. Well, I can only imagine what that is like, but if it is anything like the buzz that I get when I'm on-stage, then I can understand why they keep on doing it.

I've been doing this for over forty years, and I can't see me ever giving it up. I love what I do, and I love talking to my fans. People still stop me in the street to talk, but if they ask if I still make money from the record, "Let's Twist Again, Like We Did Last Summer," I do have to say "That was "Chubby Checker" you daft cunt! Now fuck off." But most people are fine, and on the whole, complimentary. I love people, and I love a character. That's why I watch "The Jeremy Kyle Show." It's a great place to get material for my act, because there's quite a bit of "Pond Life" on that programme. It always makes me smile when some ugly bastard with spots all over his face and three teeth in his mouth, is complaining that his girlfriend has slept with someone else. I mean, he's so ugly, he could frighten a fucking ghost, so no wonder she's been elsewhere. Then, the other bloke comes on and he looks worse that the first one did AND he has seventeen kids by seventeen different women, and doesn't work.

The downside of the job is the travelling, and I've just got back from my latest Australian tour. But this time, I flew on the new "Emirates Airways" Double Decker Airbus, which is fantastic. Planes like that make travelling much easier. I came to the conclusion that to get a job as a stewardess on Emirates, you have to be a beauty queen; I was definitely born forty years too early! Of course, I'm only joking, I am the luckiest man alive because I have a beautiful wife whom I adore, and I hate leaving her when I go away to work. You see, the trouble is that she is a terrible traveller; if I take her to Skegness, I have to stop the car four times for her to throw up.

I'll never forget the day Helen walked into my life, mainly because her tits entered the room before she did. She had a fantastic figure and beautiful eyes. I thought if I'd been twenty-five years younger, I would have made a play for her. Amazingly, something just clicked between us and we started seeing each other. We were good together, and I knew straight away that this was different to any relationship that I have had before. The age difference meant nothing to either of us; we both felt that we were meant to be together. We married in Las Vegas, and now have two beautiful children. Reece is the eldest, and he takes after his mother. He's caring, thoughtful and sensitive. Amy is more like me; she goes at everything like a bull in a china shop. She makes me laugh. In fact, the day before I flew to Australia she said, "Dad, am I coming with you?" So I had to explain to her that as it was such a long way, it would take me two days to get there. She looked at me with her big eyes and said that she wouldn't mind that, but I knew that there wasn't enough colouring books in the world to keep her occupied for that amount of time. I was worried about how she would take this, but I needn't have bothered, she just said, "OK. Don't forget to bring me some presents back." And went off to do something else.

We love our holidays with the kids, and have been going to Portugal for many years. In fact, we were there in May 2007 when Madeleine McCann disappeared. We were only twenty-five miles from Praia Da Luz where it happened. Helen and I were so upset about the news, and she, along with most parents over there became paranoid about the children's safety, so all four of us ended up sleeping in the one bed. I found myself driving around the resort looking out for anything suspicious, and looking at small children to see if they looked like Madeleine. Of course, Portugal is a vast country, so it was like looking for a needle in a haystack, but everyone tried their best. The kids obviously asked questions, and we tried our best to explain in a way they could understand, but we all were very upset, and felt so sorry for that family. I still think about Madeleine, and relive that holiday thinking that it could have been one of our kids. It's so sad.

# *In Conclusion*

Well, you've nearly reached the end of this book, and I hope you've enjoyed reading it. It's been good taking this trip down memory lane, I've led an "interesting" life and it's been good to share some of the stories with you. I've had great success as Britain's bluest comedian, and that success has taken me all over the world. I have made a fair amount of money doing this, and have also paid out for a very expensive divorce. I still have fond memories of the days when I played drums in a band, and I loved the camaraderie between the acts in those working men's clubs. I feel lucky to have travelled the world in the merchant navy at such a young age. But most of all, I am now very happy and settled in my private life. But some things do need to be put straight.

As the man that was dubbed the rudest, crudest, bluest, sexist, racist, homophobic man in the country, I have been blamed for many things. I have had to live under a cloud for the last forty years. You see, people like to pin the blame on me for things that I am supposed to have said and done, but the time is right for me to put a few things straight. I have been accused of saying some pretty awful things at the most inappropriate of times. Some of these things have been quite witty when you look back, but I just didn't say them. Things become accepted as fact if they are repeated enough times, and we do things just because we're told that is what you have to do. I mean, the Bible doesn't say that we should bring a tree inside and light it up with fairy lights at Christmas, but we do. Jesus didn't feel that he had to make an emergency trip to the garage to get a last minute Christmas present for someone he forgot, but we've all done that. The band on the Titanic surely didn't actually carry on playing when the stage was at a ninety-five degree angle. And whilst we're at it, Ronald Biggs wasn't the ringleader of the Great Train Robbers; people just think he was because he was the one that got all the press coverage when he escaped to Rio. These are all things that we do, or that we believe to be true because somebody told us. It may be true that I have considered having an inscription on my gravestone saying, "I'm laying here waiting for you all to Fuck Off." But I do need to put a few things straight.

Firstly, during the Falklands War, I NEVER said (at a bad gig,) "I'm going down like the HMS Sheffield."

# Don't blame me, says angry comic

CONTROVERSIAL clubland comedian Roy Chubby Brown is big enough to admit when he's fluffed a gag . . .

But the latest rumour sweeping Teesside has him fuming.

The comic has received abusive telephone calls and been stopped in the street by angry club members.

### Rumour

The rumour is that he said during an act earlier this week that his jokes "were going down like the Sheffield."

But Chubby denies saying it. "I'm getting tired of being blamed for this one. There's

**CHUBBY BROWN**
'Tired of blame'

no bigger Royalist in the town than me.

"It all started after I appeared at the Acklam Garden City Club on Monday when a scuffle broke out.

Now the story is going around that I was involved and the cheap crack about the Sheffield was at the centre of it."

A late-night telephone call to his home by someone who had picked up the rumour has now forced the comic to have his number changed.

### 'Not me'

"I always seem to get the blame when these stories go round. This time I want to make it clear I never said anything of the sort."

Acklam Garden City Club committee member Phil Atkinson: "I was in the club on Monday and Chubby made no reference at all to the Sheffield.

"In fact, his act went down very well and he got a great reception."

Secondly, after the child sex abuse scandal in my home town of Middlesbrough, where over a hundred children were taken away from their families because some doctor misdiagnosed sexual abuse by parents. I definitely DIDN'T say, "I'm surprised to see so many people here tonight, I thought that you'd all be at home fucking your kids."

Thirdly, I DID NOT walk on stage at a catholic club in the north-east (that had been broken into the night before) and point to the large crucifix on the wall and say, "I see you got the cunt who stole your telly." I know who did say this one, and he has been mentioned in this book several times. He was a comedian whom I greatly admired.

Fourthly, I am not racist or homophobic. "Chubby" the character might be, but he is more of a caricature of some of the bigots that really exist in this country. I do have concerns about the number of people that have got into the UK illegally, and I can't say I'm too happy about whole areas that have become like middle-eastern strongholds, where women are made to cover their faces. To me, that is totally alien to all that is British. It seems to me that the women in these societies get a very raw deal, which is totally wrong. Britain is a great place to live, and people have died for the freedom that we have in this country. I really don't have a problem with anyone who embraces the British way of life and who wants to be part of our society. I do have a problem with people who want to destroy our way of life, and think that those who want to preach hatred of the west really don't belong in a western country.

With regards to my so-called homophobia, all I can say is that I am neither frightened, or hate anyone because of who they choose to sleep with. I maybe don't understand them, but I don't hate them.

But the story that probably gets told the most is that shortly after the tragic fire at Bradford's Valley Parade ground. I am supposed to have said (at a gig in Bradford,) "I'm upset that you didn't invite me to the barbecue." I categorically DID NOT say this. Fifty-six people died on that day, and more than two hundred and sixty five people were injured. Like most normal people, I was shocked and upset at how many people lost their lives. There is no way on earth that I could ever have made a joke about it, especially in Bradford. I may be daft, but I'm not stupid, I would have got lynched.

I do understand that I have created a character that could have said these things, but I defy anybody to truthfully say that they were at the show when I said any these things, because if they did, they would be lying. Some things are just too sensitive, even for me. I mean, I might as well say that I go looking for cars with a "Baby on Board" sign in them, and then run them off the road! I admit that I do think of funny things to say about the news, but I couldn't be that cruel. In fact, when Princess Diana died, we cancelled the show in Blackpool that night. Jokes and text messages were flying around, but I took the view that I just couldn't say anything on stage, as the public outpouring of grief was immense. It took me six months before I dare mention it. So please give me a bit of credit, I might be crude, but I'm not cruel.

I got into comedy after reading a book in prison called, "I Owe Russia Two Thousand Dollars" by Bob Hope. It included photos of him standing in front of thousand of laughing GI's, and I thought, "I'd like to do that." In fact, that book helped me to grow up, and I realised that there was more to life than counting bricks in a cell or losing my temper and getting into fights over the least little thing.

So, in conclusion, I'd like to thank Bob Hope for that book, because it changed the path my life was taking. I'd also like to thank everyone who has been part of my life. I'd like to thank my parents, without whom I wouldn't be here. I would also thank all my mates in the merchant navy and those from my band days. I certainly wouldn't like to thank all those bastard concert chairmen, because a lot of them were twats. But I would like to thank a few of the people who helped me in the early days, but died far too young: Brian Findlay, Ronnie Keegan, Kay Rouselle and Anne Maddison. I would also like to mention Peter Richardson, John Yorke, Tony "Banger" Walsh, Mick Sheppard, Ritchie Hoyle and Arran Culpan. These were the guys who worked with me to make "Chubby Brown" one of the biggest selling theatre acts in Britain. I would like to thank my manager, Stuart Littlewood and everyone at Handshake Group for their hard work.

Finally, I have to thank Steve Cowper who worked with me for many years. We are still great friends, and he has helped me write this book. His memory is better than mine!

I would like to dedicate this book to my loving wife Helen, and our wonderful children, Reece and Amy.

Thank you for taking the time to read these stories, I hope that you have enjoyed them, and maybe learned a bit about me that you didn't know before.